Carta's

ISRAEL

Road Atlas

CARTA
JERUSALEM

CONTENTS

Key Map III
Legend to **Road Atlas** - Map of Israel · · · IV
Legend to City Maps V
Road Atlas - Map of Israel 1-58
Map of Jerusalem 59-62
Map of Tel Aviv 63-68
Index to City Maps 69-74
Index to **Road Atlas** - Map of Israel · · 75-91

Scale: **Road Atlas** 1:160,000

```
0   1   2   3   4   5                    10
                                            km
                                     miles
0     1     2     3     4     5
```

Reception of Radio Channels by Area

Area	Maps
Galilee Panhandle	1-2
Tzfat (Safad)	3-4, 5-6
Haifa	7-8, 11-12
Beit She'an Valley	9-10, 13-14
Center, Greater Tel Aviv	15-16, 21-22, 27-28
Jerusalem	17-18, 19-20, 23-24, 25-26
Beersheba	27-28, 29-30, 31-32, 33-34, 35-36
Northern Negev	37-38, 39-40, 41-42, 43-44, 47-48
Arava	45-46, 49-50
Eilat	51-52, 53-54, 55-56, 57-58

Designed and prepared by **Carta**, Jerusalem
Great care has been taken to ensure that the information
contained in this Atlas is accurate and up-to-date. However,
the Publishers cannot be responsible for any consequences
arising from errors, omissions or misleading information.

ISBN: 978-965-220-783-8
Printed in Israel

carta@carta.co.il
www.carta.co.il
18 Ha'uman Street, P.O.B. 2500, Jerusalem 91024
Tel: 02-6783355   Fax: 02-6782373

KEY
MAP

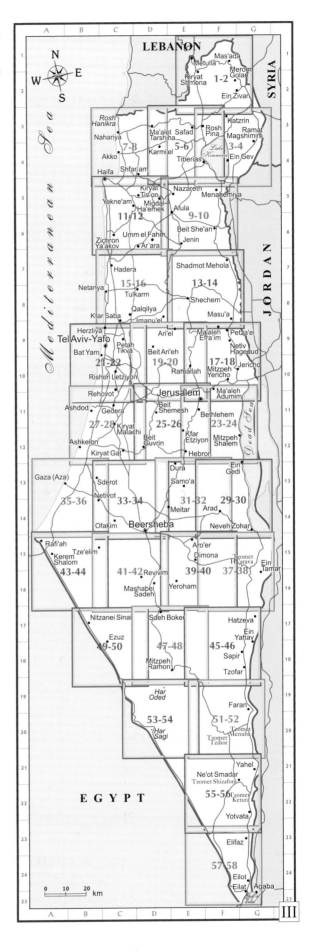

III

LEGEND TO MAP OF ISRAEL

Under construction
6 Road No. 6 (Toll Road) (trans-Israel highway)

Motorway Interchange
4 Two-lane highway and road number

89 Main highway and number
Single lane · Two-lane

886 Regional road and number
Single lane · Two-lane

Local road

Other road

Road in planning, under construction

Main access route, in Judea & Samaria (Due to changing circumstances check before traveling.)

Unpaved road

Junctions
12 Distance in km between junctions
Distance

"Israel Footpath"

Bridge, railway line, station

City or town built-up area

○ Town, village or settlement

◉ Jewish town, village or settlement in Judea & Samaria

■ Other named site

⊖ No entry

Reservoir or fish pond

● Well, spring

Stream: perennial; intermittent

Sands, sand dunes

Forest

Nature reserve

✈ Airport, landing strip

Site with archaeological remains

★ Other site of interest

✳ Scenic site

Lookout point

Field School (Field study center S.P.N.I.)

Monument, memorial

Bathing beach

Park, national park

Picnic spot

⚠ Camping, overnight camp

Hotel, holiday resort, hostel

∴ Ruin

∩ Cave

International boundary

1974 Separation of Forces line

Security fence

Planned

Palestinian Autonomous area

Area A

Area B

Nature reserve

Warning

If in doubt about the safety of a place or route, the whereabouts of IDF firing zones etc., it is necessary to check with the relevant authorities wherever possible. In any event it is recommended to seek information from the Nature Reserves & National Parks Authority, the Nature Preservation Society and branches of the Keren Kayemet located throughout the country.

IV

LEGEND TO CITY MAPS

Inter-city highway		Park, gardens
Main artery		Forest, woods, orchards
Major 2-lane street		Intermittent stream
Main street		Illuminated site
Other street		Tourist information
One-way street		Central bus station
Pedestrian mall		Railway station
Footpath		Lookout point
Unpaved road		Museum
Railway		Hospital
Municipal boundary		Magen David Adom
Parking		Stadium
Tunnel, bridge, pedestrian bridge		Hotel
Public building		Embassy, consulate
Built-up area		Police station
Jewish cemetery		Gas station
Muslim cemetery		Post office
Christian cemetery		Synagogue
		Other site

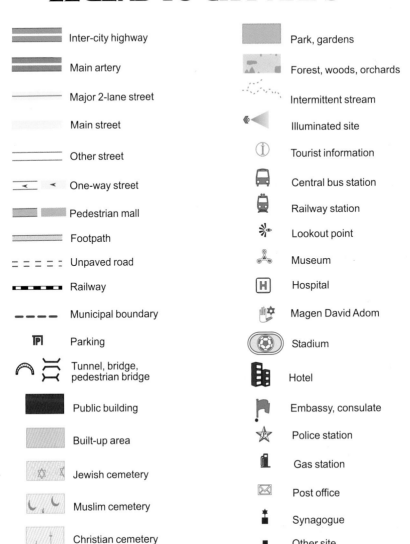

V

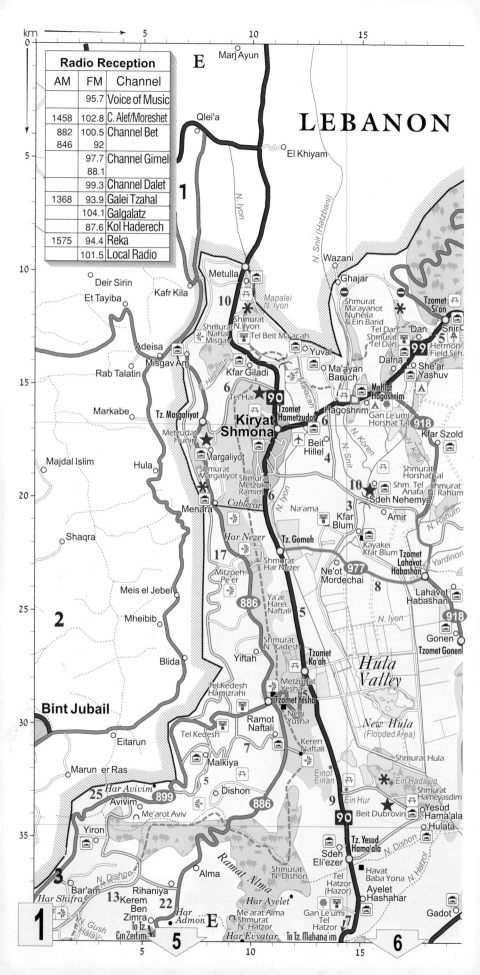

LEBANON

AM	FM	Channel
	95.7	Voice of Music
1458	102.8	C. Alef/Moreshet
882	100.5	Channel Bet
846	92	
	97.7	Channel Gimel
	88.1	
	99.3	Channel Dalet
1368	93.9	Galei Tzahal
	104.1	Galgalatz
	87.6	Kol Haderech
1575	94.4	Reka
	101.5	Local Radio

Radio Reception

Marj Ayun

Qlei'a

El Khiyam

Wazani

Ghajar

Tzomet Si'on

N. Snir (Hatzbani)

N. Iyon

Deir Sirin

Kafr Kila

Et Tayiba

Metulla

Mapalei N. Iyon

Shmurat Ma'ayanot Nuheila & Ein Barid

Dan

Snir

Shmurat N. Iyon

Shmurat Tel Dan

Hermon Field Sch.

Adeisa

Nahal Misgav

Shmurat Misgav

Tel Beit Ma'acah

Yuval

Ma'ayan Baruch

Tel Dan

Dafna

She'ar Yashuv

Misgav Am

Kfar Giladi

Mehola Hagoshrim

Rab Talatin

Tz. Margaliyot

Tel Hai

Tzomet Hametzudot

Hagoshrim

Gan Le'umi Horshat Tal

Kfar Szold

Markabe

Kiryat Shmona

Beit Hillel

Majdal Islim

Hula

Metzudat Hunin

Margaliyot

Shmurat Horshat Tal

Shmurat Margaliyot

Shmurat Metzukei Ramim

Na'ama

Shm. Tel Anafa

Shmurat N. Rahum

Menara

Cablecar

N. Iyon

Kfar Blum

Sdeh Nehemya

Amir

N. Rahum

Shaqra

Har Nezer

Tz. Gomeh

Kayakei Kfar Blum

Tzomet Lahavot Habashan

Yardinon

Mitzpeh Pe'er

Shmurat Har Nezer

Ne'ot Mordechai

Lahavot Habashan

Meis el Jebel

Ya'ar Harei Naftali

N. Iyon

Gonen

Mheibib

Shmurat N. Kadesh

Tzomet Ko'ah

Hula Valley

Tzomet Gonen

Blida

Yiftah

Bint Jubail

Tel Kedesh Hamizrahi

Metzudat Yesha

Tzomet Yesha

New Hula (Flooded Area)

Eitarun

Tel Kedesh

Ramot Naftali

Nebi Yusha

Keren Naftali

Shmurat Hula

Marun er Ras

Malkiya

Einot Einan

Ein Hadayig

Shmurat Hameyasdim

Har Avivim

Dishon

Yesud Hama'ala

Avivim

Me'arot Aviv

Ein Hur

Beit Dubrovin

Hulata

Yiron

Tz. Yesud Hama'ala

N. Dishon

Bar'am

Alma

Sdeh Eli'ezer

Havat Baba Yona

Har Shifra

Rihaniya

Ramat Alma

Shmurat N. Dishon

Tel Hatzor (Hazor)

Ayelet Hashahar

Kerem Ben Zimra

Har Admon

Har Ayelet

Me'arat Alma Shmurat N. Hatzor

Gan Le'umi Tel Hatzor

Gadot

Ein Zeitim

Har Evyatar

To Tz. Mahana'im

To Tz.

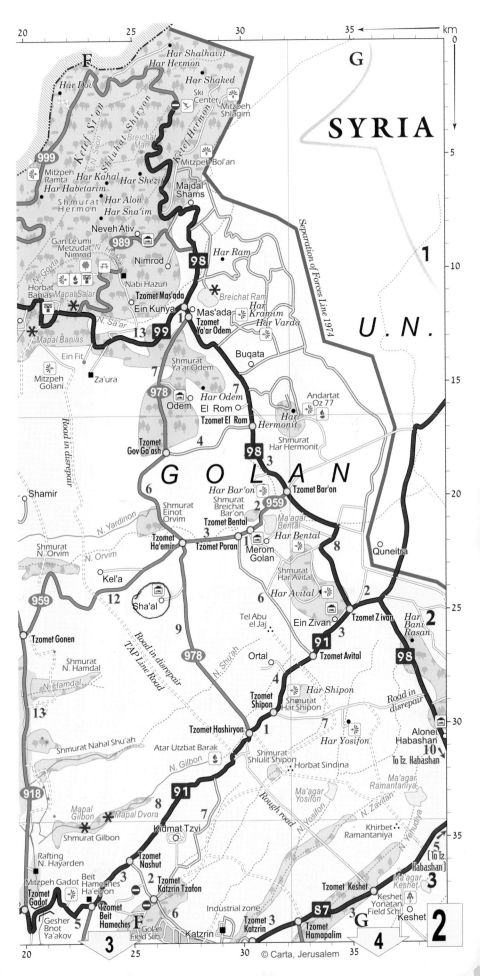

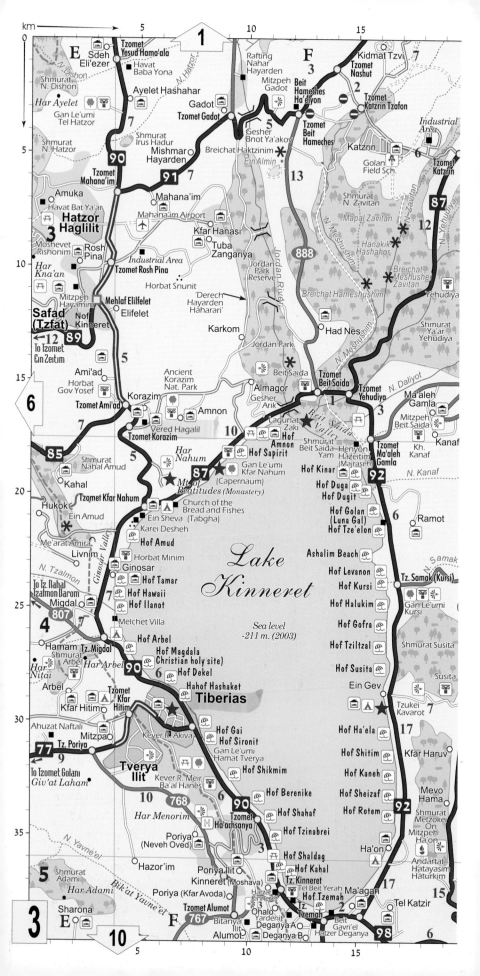

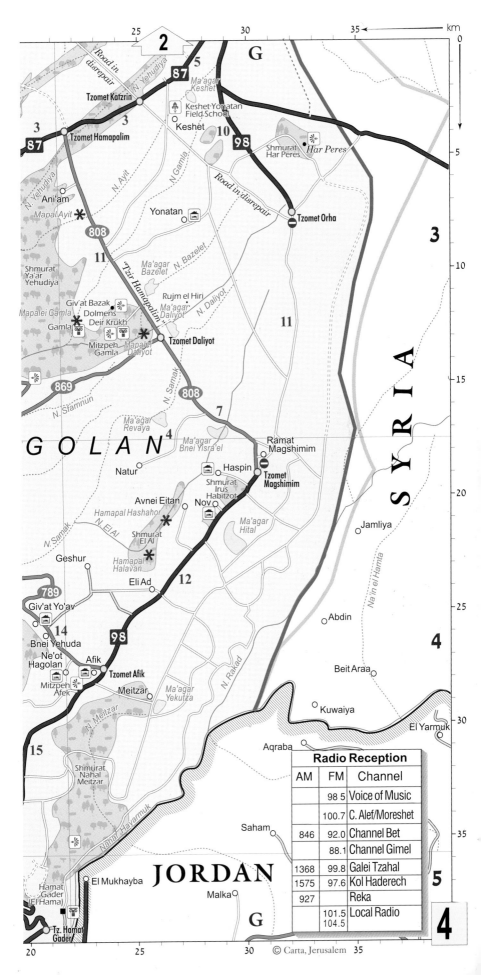

2

25   30   35 ◄   — km
                                    0

G

Road in disrepair

N. Yehudiya

87   5

Tzomet Katzrin   Ma'agar Keshet

Keshet Yonatan Field School

3   3
87   Keshet   10   98
Tzomet Hamapalim   Shmurat Har Peres • *Har Peres*   5

N. Yehudiya

Ani'am
Mapal Ayit ✳   Road in disrepair
808   Yonatan
                                    Tzomet Orha   3

N. Ayit

11   N. Gamla

Shmurat Ya'ar Yehudiya   Ma'agar Bazelet   N. Bazelet
                                            10

Mapalei Gamla   Giv'at Bazak • Dolmens   Rujm el Hiri
✳   Deir Krukh   Ma'agar Daliyot   N. Daliyot
Gamla   ✳ ✳   11
Mitzpeh Gamla   Mapalei Daliyot ✳ Tzomet Daliyot

869   N. Samak
                                            15
N. Sfamnun   808

G O L A N   7   N. Samak

Ma'agar Revaya   4
Natur   Ma'agar Bnei Yisra'el   Ramat Magshimim

Haspin ○   Tzomet Magshimim
Shmurat Irus Habitzot   ⊖
Avnei Eitan   Nov ○   20
Hamapal Hashahor ✳   Ma'agar Hital
N. El Al   Shmurat El Al
N. Samak   ✳
Geshur   *Hamapal Halavan* ✳   Jamliya ○

Eli Ad   12   **S Y R I A**
789
Giv'at Yo'av   Na'in el Hamia
14   25
Bnei Yehuda   Abdin ○
Ne'ot Hagolan   98   4
Afik
Mitzpeh Afek   Tzomet Afik   Beit Araa ○
Meitzar   Ma'agar Yekutza
N. Meitzar   N. Rakad
                                            30
15   Kuwaiya ○
                                    El Yarmuk ○

Shmurat Nahal Meitzar   Aqraba ○

Radio Reception		
AM	FM	Channel
	98 5	Voice of Music
	100.7	C. Alef/Moreshet
846	92.0	Channel Bet
	88.1	Channel Gimel
1368	99.8	Galei Tzahal
1575	97.6	Kol Haderech
927		Reka
	101.5 104.5	Local Radio

Nahar Hayarmuk   Saham ○   35

JORDAN

Hamat Gader (El Hama)   El Mukhayba ○
                                    Malka ○   5
Tz. Hamat Gader   **G**

20   25   30   © Carta, Jerusalem 35

4

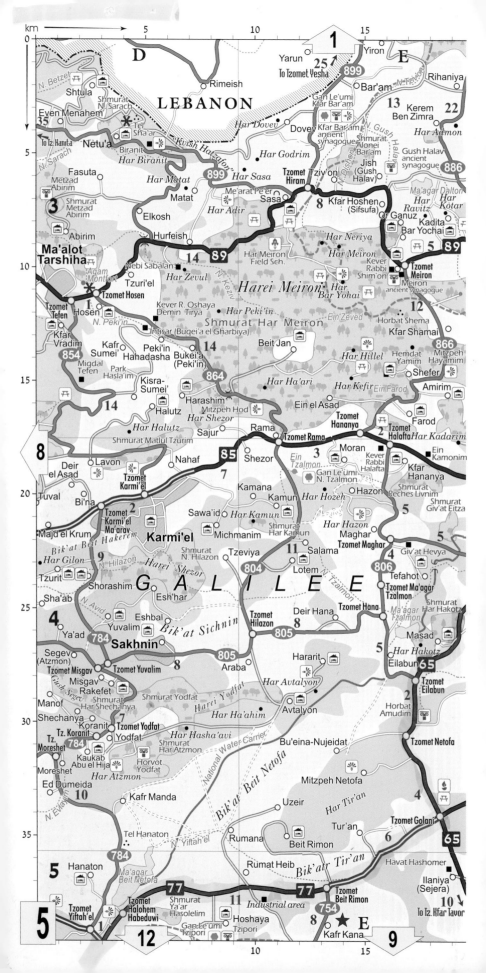

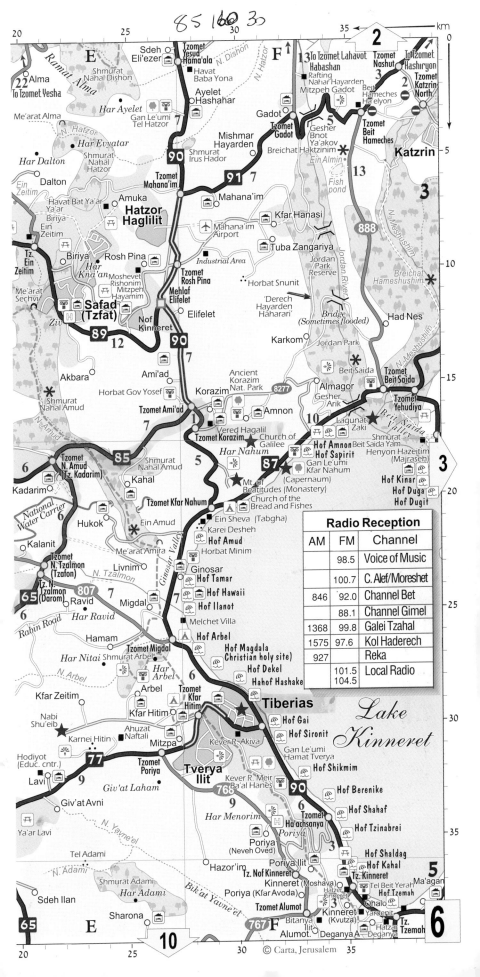

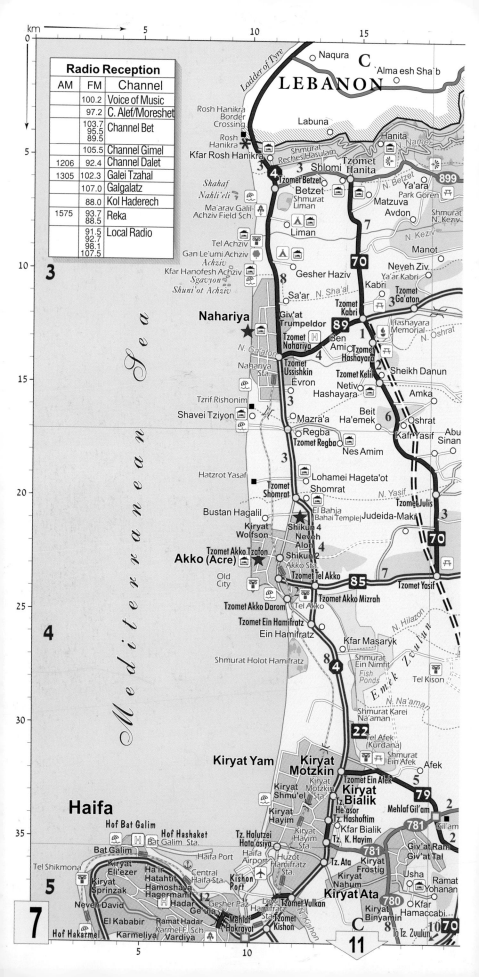

Radio Reception

AM	FM	Channel
	100.2	Voice of Music
	97.2	C. Alef/Moreshet
	103.7 95.5 89.5	Channel Bet
	105.5	Channel Gimel
1206	92.4	Channel Dalet
1305	102.3	Galei Tzahal
	107.0	Galgalatz
	88.0	Kol Haderech
1575	93.7 88.5	Reka
	91.5 92.7 98.1 107.5	Local Radio

km

5 · 10 · 15

C

Naqura

LEBANON

Alma esh Sha'b

Ladder of Tyre

Rosh Hanikra Border Crossing

Labuna

Hanita

N. Namer

Rosh Hanikra

Shmurat Reches Hasulam

Kfar Rosh Hanikra

Shlomi

Tzomet Hanita

4

Tzomet Betzet

Ya'ara

Park Goren

899

Shahaf Nahli'eli

Betzet

Shmurat Liman

Matzuva

Avdon

Shmurat N. Keziv

3

Ma'arav Galil-Achziv Field Sch.

Liman

N. Keziv

Manot

Tel Achziv

Gan Le'umi Achziv

Achziv

Kfar Hanofesh Achziv

Sgavyon

Shuni'ot Achziv

8

Gesher Haziv

Neveh Ziv

70

Ya'ar Kabri

Sa'ar

N. Sha'al

Kabri

Tzomet Ga'aton

3

Nahariya

Giv'at Trumpeldor

Tzomet Kabri

Hashayara Memorial

89

N. Oshrat

Tzomet Nahariya

Ben Ami

Tzomet Hashayara

1

N. Ga'aton

4

Tzomet Ussishkin

Tzomet Kelil

Sheikh Danun

2

Nahariya Sta.

Evron

Netiv Hashayara

Amka

Tzrif Rishonim

Tzomet Regba

Mazra'a

Beit Ha'emek

6

Oshrat

Shavei Tziyon

3

Kafr Yasif

Abu Sinan

Regba

Nes Amim

3

Hatzrot Yasaf

Lohamei Hageta'ot

Shomrat

N. Yasif

Tzomet Julis

3

Tzomet Shomrat

El Bahja (Bahai Temple)

Judeida-Makr

70

Bustan Hagalil

Shikun 4

Neveh Alon

4

Kiryat Wolfson

Shikun 2

Akko Sta.

Akko (Acre)

Tzomet Akko Tzafon

Tzomet Tel Akko

85

Tzomet Yasif

7

Old City

Tzomet Akko Mizrah

Tzomet Akko Darom

Tel Akko

Tzomet Ein Hamifratz

Kfar Masaryk

N. Hilazon

Ein Hamifratz

Shmurat Holot Hamifratz

8

4

Shmurat Ein Nimfit

Fish Ponds

Tel Kison

E m e k Z v u l u n

Shmurat Karei Na'aman

N. Na'aman

22

Tel Afek (Kurdana)

Shmurat Ein'Afek

Kiryat Yam

Kiryat Motzkin

Afek

Kiryat Motzkin Sta.

Tzomet Ein Afek

5

Kiryat Shmu'el

Kiryat Bialik

Mehlaf Gil'am

79

2

Haifa

Kiryat Hayim

He'asor

Tz. Hashoftim

Kfar Bialik

781

Gil'am

Giv'at Ram

Giv'at Tal

2

Hof Bat Galim

Hof Hashaket

Bat Galim Sta.

Kiryat Hayim Sta.

Tz. K. Hayim

781

Kiryat Frostig

Usha

Ramat Yohanan

Bat Galim

Tz. Halutzei Hata'asiya

Haifa Airport

Huzot Hamifratz Sta.

Tz. Ata

Kiryat Nahum

Tel Shikmona

Kiryat Eli'ezer

Kiryat Sprinzak

Ha'ir Hatahtit Hamoshava Hagermanit

Central Haifa Sta.

Kishon Port

Lev Hamifratz Sta.

Kiryat Ata

Kfar Hamaccabi

Neveh David

Hadar

Ge'ula

Gesher Paz

Tzomet Vulkan

Kiryat Binyamin

780

70

El Kababir

Ramat Hadar

Karmel F. Sch.

Mehlaf Hakrayot

Tzomet Kishon

8

To Tz. Zvulun

10

Hof Hakarmel

Karmeliya

Vardiya

C

11

M e d i t e r r a n e a n S e a

3

4

5

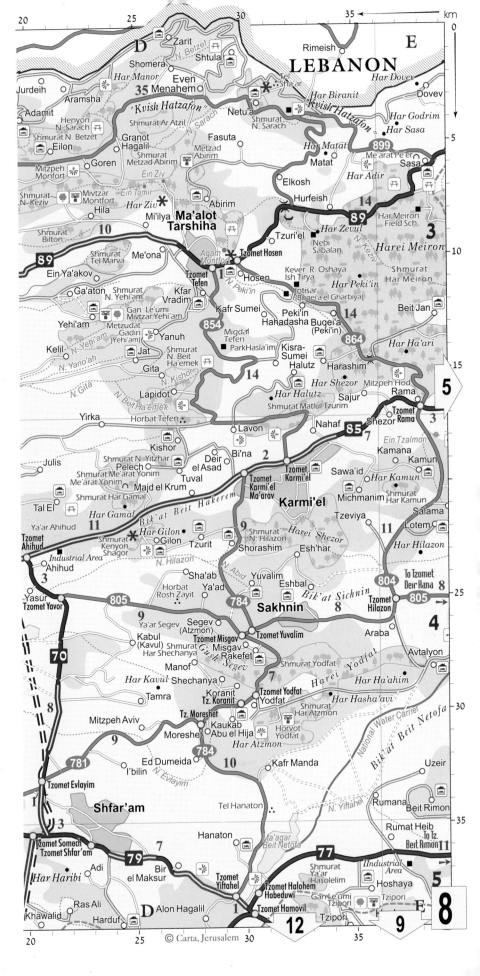

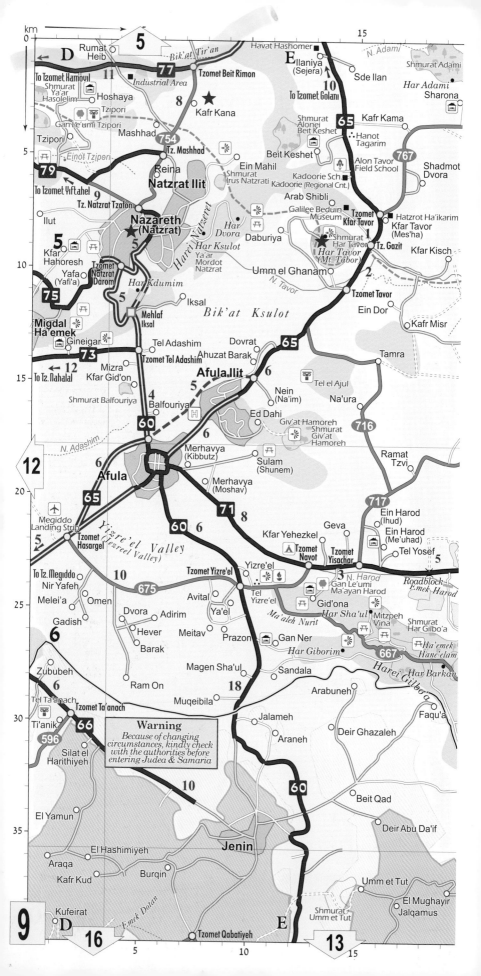

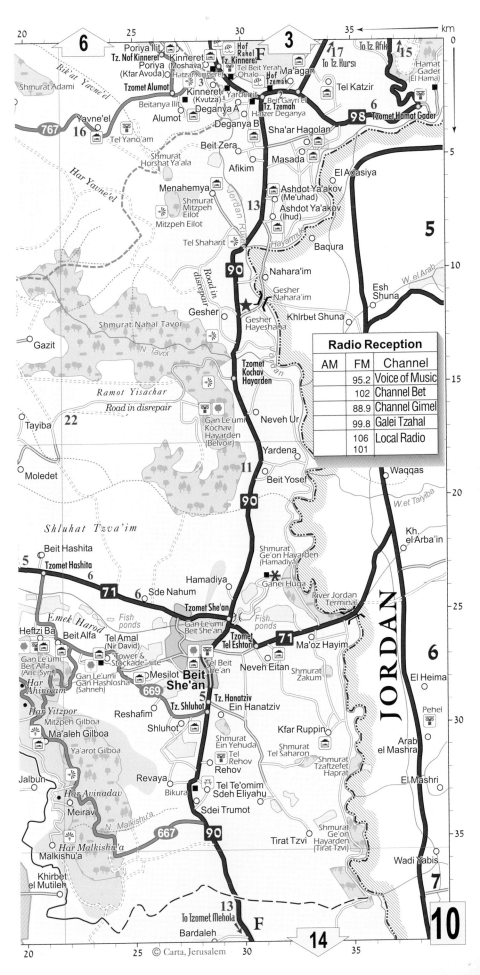

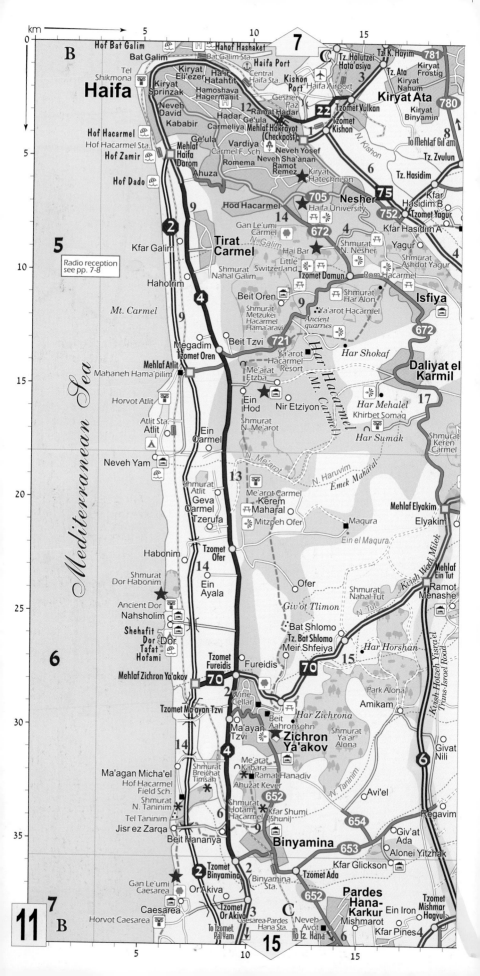

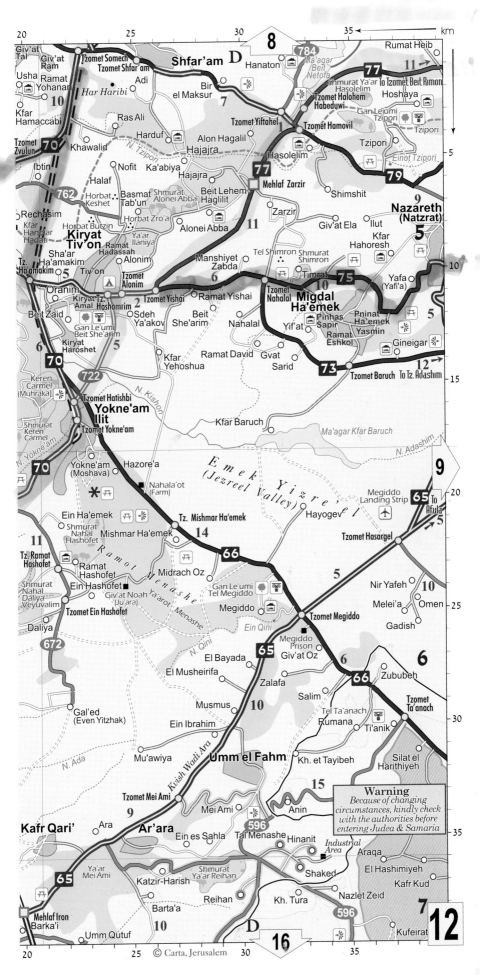

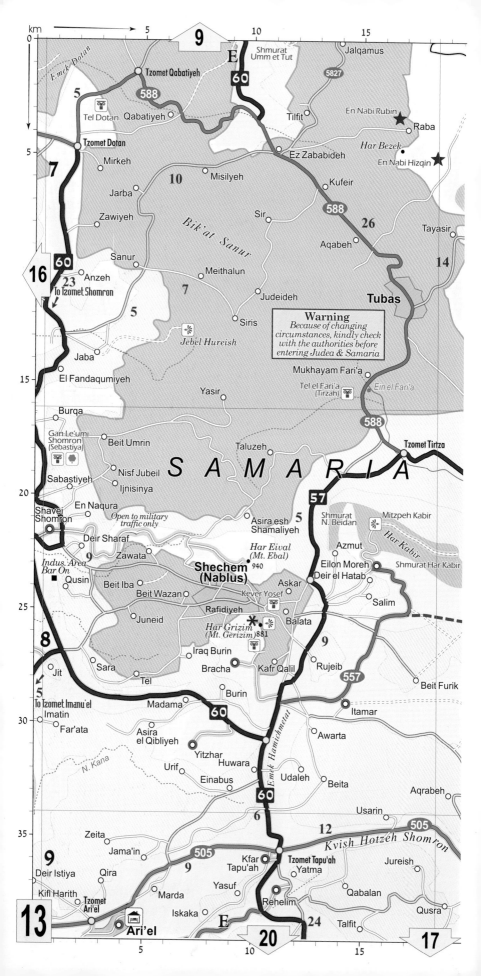

km
0
5
10
15

9

E
60

Shmurat
Umm et Tut

Jalqamus

5827

Emek Dotan

Tzomet Qabatiyeh
588
5
Tel Dotan
Qabatiyeh

Tilfit

En Nabi Rubin ★
Raba

Har Bezek
En Nabi Hizqin ★

Tzomet Dotan
7

Mirkeh

Ez Zababideh

10
Misilyeh

Kufeir

588

Jarba

26
Tayasir

Zawiyeh

Sir

14

Bik'at Sanur

Sanur

Aqabeh

16
60
23
Anzeh
To Tzomet Shomron

Meithalun

7

Judeideh

Tubas

5

Siris

Warning
*Because of changing
circumstances, kindly check
with the authorities before
entering Judea & Samaria*

Jebel Hureish

Jaba

Yasir

Mukhayam Fari'a

Ein el Fari'a

El Fandaqumiyeh

Tel el Fari'a
(Tirzah)

588

Burqa

Beit Umrin

Taluzeh

S A M A R I A

Tzomet Tirtza

Gan Le'umi
Shomron
(Sebastiya)

Nisf Jubeil

Sabastiyeh

Ijnisinya

En Naqura

57

Shmurat
N. Beidan

Mitzpeh Kabir

Shavei
Shomron

*Open to military
traffic only*

Asira esh
Shamaliyeh
5

Azmut

Har Kabir

Deir Sharaf

Har Eival
(Mt. Ebal)
940

Eilon Moreh

Shmurat Har Kabir

9

Zawata

Indus. Area
Bar On

Qusin

Beit Iba

**Shechem
(Nablus)**

Askar

Deir el Hatab

Salim

Beit Wazan

Kever Yosef

Juneid

Rafidiyeh

Balata

9

Har Grizim
(Mt. Gerizim) 881

Kafr Qalil

Rujeib

557

8

Jit

Sara

Iraq Burin

Bracha

Beit Furik

5
To Tzomet Imanu'el
Imatin

Tel

Burin

Itamar

Madama

60

Far'ata

N. Kana

Asira
el Qibliyeh

Yitzhar

Huwara

Awarta

Urif

Udaleh

Beita

Einabus

Aqrabeh

60
6

Usarin

505

Zeita

Jama'in

12

Kvish Hotzeh Shomron

505

9

Deir Istiya

Qira

505
9

Kfar
Tapu'ah

Tzomet Tapu'ah
Yatma

Jureish

Kifl Harith

Marda

Yasuf

Qabalan

Qusra

13

Tzomet
Ari'el

Iskaka

Rehelim

Ari'el

E

5

10

20

24

Talfit

17

Emek Hamichmetal

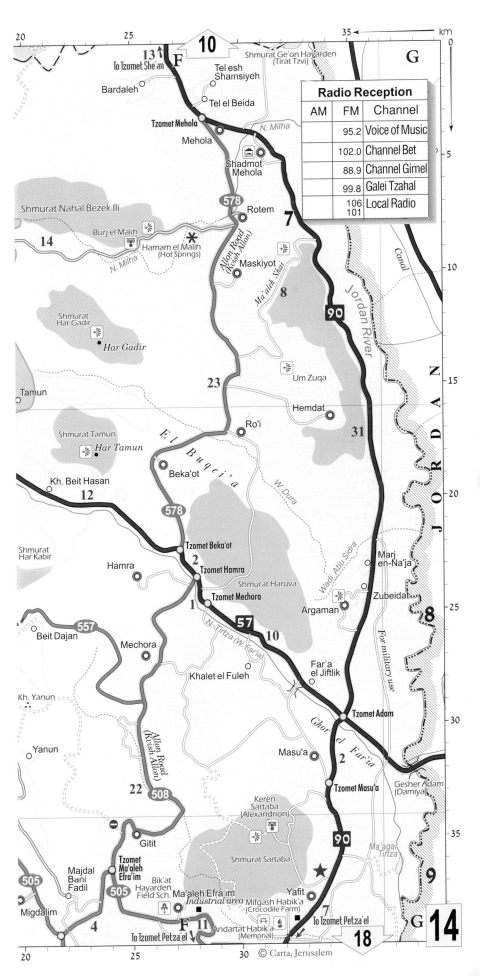

Radio Reception

AM	FM	Channel
	95.2	Voice of Music
	102.0	Channel Bet
	88.9	Channel Gimel
	99.8	Galei Tzahal
	106 101	Local Radio

km

20
25
35
10
G
F

13 To Tzomet She'an
Shmurat Ge'on Hayarden (Tirat Tzvi)
Bardaleh
Tel esh Shamsiyeh
Tel el Beida
Tzomet Mehola
Mehola
N. Milha
5
Shadmot Mehola
578
Rotem
7
Shmurat Nahal Bezek Ili
14
Burj el Malih
Hamam el Malih (Hot Springs)
Allon Road (Kvish Allon)
Maskiyot
Ma'aleh Shai
10
8
90
Jordan River
Shmurat Har Gadir
Har Gadir
23
Um Zuqa
Canal
15
Hemdat
31
Tamun
Ro'i
El Buqei'a
Shmurat Tamun
Har Tamun
Beka'ot
W. Dura
20
Kh. Beit Hasan
12
578
JORDAN
Shmurat Har Kabir
Tzomet Beka'ot
2
Marj en-Na'ja
Hamra
Tzomet Hamra
Shmurat Haruva
Wadi Abu Sidra
Zubeidat
8
1
Tzomet Mechora
Argaman
Beit Dajan
557
N. Tirtza (W. Far'a)
57
10
25
Mechora
Khalet el Fuleh
Far'a el Jiftlik
For military use
Kh. Yanun
Ghor el Far'ia
Tzomet Adam
30
Yanun
Masu'a
2
22
508
Allon Road (Kvish Allon)
Tzomet Masu'a
Gesher Adam (Damiya)
Gitit
Keren Sartaba (Alexandrion)
35
Majdal Bani Fadil
Tzomet Ma'aleh Efra'im
Bik'at Hayarden Field Sch.
Ma'aleh Efra'im Industrial area
Shmurat Sartaba
Ma'agan Tirtza
505
505
Mifgash Habik'a (Crocodile Farm)
Yafit
90
9
Migdalim
4
F
11
Andartat Habik'a (Memorial)
To Tzomet Petza'el
7
To Tzomet Petza'el
G
14
To Tzomet Petza'el
18
© Carta, Jerusalem

20
25
30
35

© Carta, Jerusalem

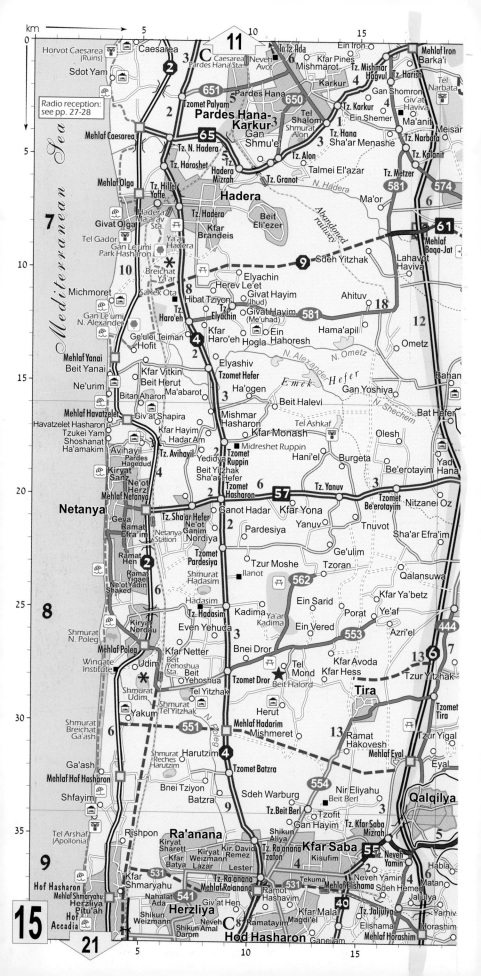

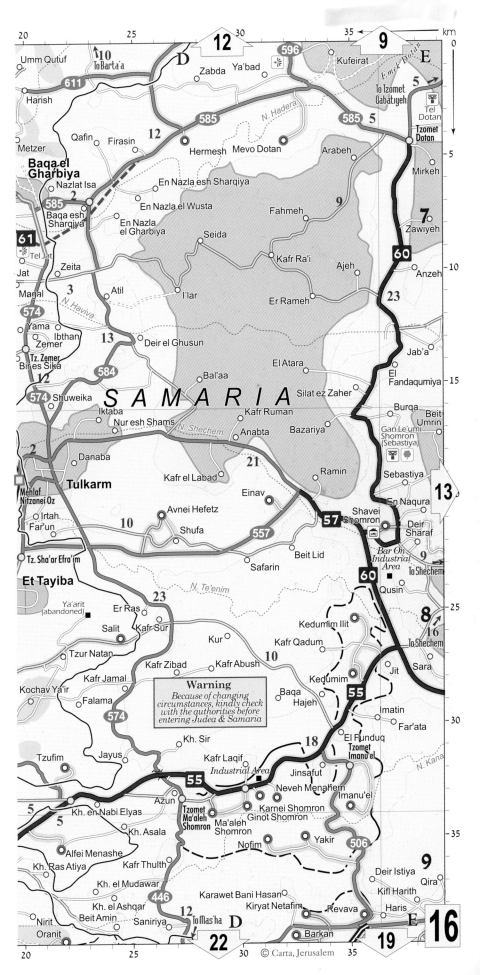

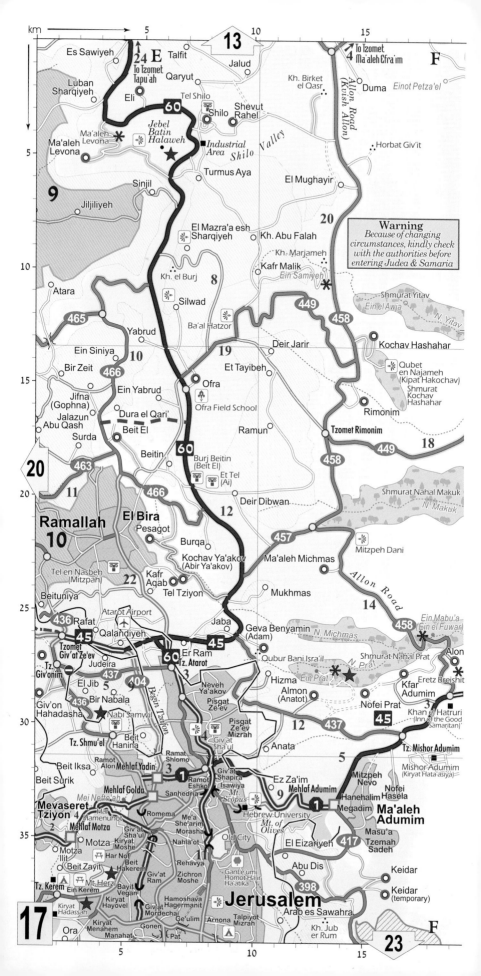

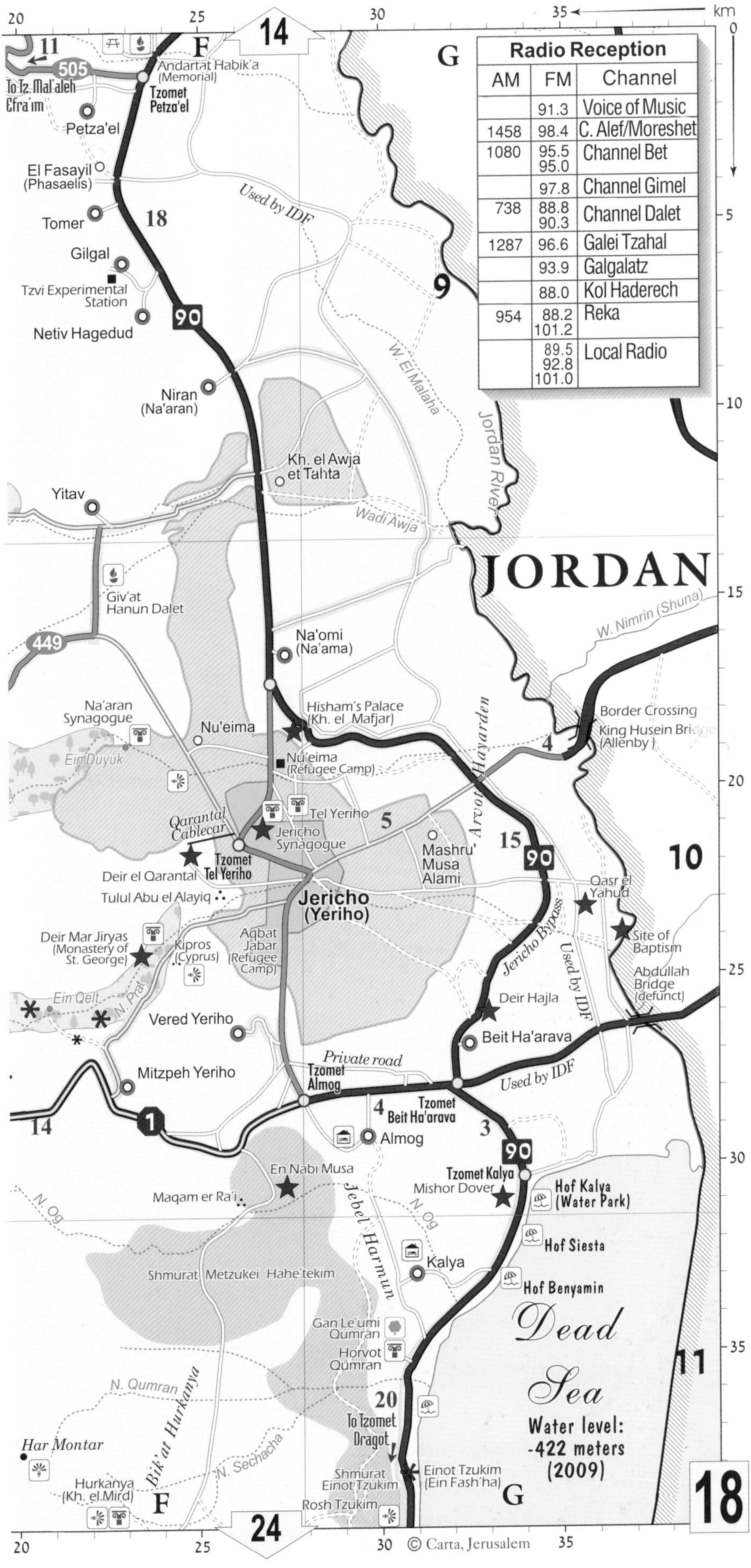
14
24
F
G
km
To Tz. Mal'aleh Efra'im
505
11
Andartat Habik'a (Memorial)
Tzomet Petza'el
Petza'el
El Fasayil (Phasaelis)
Tomer
18
Gilgal
Tzvi Experimental Station
Netiv Hagedud
90
Used by IDF
9
W. El Malaha
Jordan River
Niran (Na'aran)
Kh. el Awja et Tahta
Yitav
Wadi Awja
JORDAN
Giv'at Hanun Dalet
W. Nimrin (Shuna)
449
Na'omi (Na'ama)
Na'aran Synagogue
Nu'eima
Hisham's Palace (Kh. el Mafjar)
Border Crossing
King Husein Bridge (Allenby)
4
Ein Duyuk
Nu'eima (Refugee Camp)
Arvot Hayarden
Tel Yeriho
Qarantal Cablecar
Jericho Synagogue
5
Mashru' Musa Alami
15
10
Tzomet Tel Yeriho
Deir el Qarantal
Tulul Abu el Alayiq
Jericho (Yeriho)
Qasr el Yahud
Jericho Bypass
Site of Baptism
Deir Mar Jiryas (Monastery of St. George)
Kipros (Cyprus)
Aqbat Jabar (Refugee Camp)
Used by IDF
Abdullah Bridge (defunct)
Ein Qelt
N. Prat
Deir Hajla
Vered Yeriho
Beit Ha'arava
Private road
Mitzpeh Yeriho
Tzomet Almog
Used by IDF
14
1
4
Tzomet Beit Ha'arava
3
Almog
90
En Nabi Musa
Tzomet Kalya
Mishor Dover
Hof Kalya (Water Park)
Maqam er Ra'i
N. Og
Jebel Harmun
N. Og
Hof Siesta
Kalya
Shmurat Metzukei Hahe'tekim
Hof Benyamin
Dead Sea
Gan Le'umi Qumran
Horvot Qumran
N. Qumran
Bik'at Hurkanya
20
To Tzomet Dragot
Water level: -422 meters (2009)
Har Montar
N. Sechacha
Einot Tzukim (Ein Fash'ha)
Shmurat Einot Tzukim
Hurkanya (Kh. el Mird)
Rosh Tzukim
© Carta, Jerusalem

Radio Reception

AM	FM	Channel
	91.3	Voice of Music
1458	98.4	C. Alef/Moreshet
1080	95.5 95.0	Channel Bet
	97.8	Channel Gimel
738	88.8 90.3	Channel Dalet
1287	96.6	Galei Tzahal
	93.9	Galgalatz
	88.0	Kol Haderech
954	88.2 101.2	Reka
	89.5 92.8 101.0	Local Radio

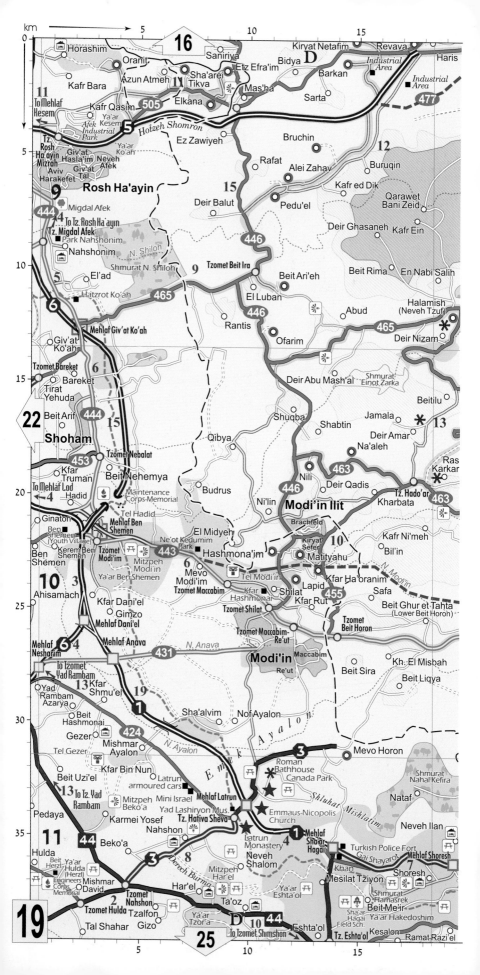

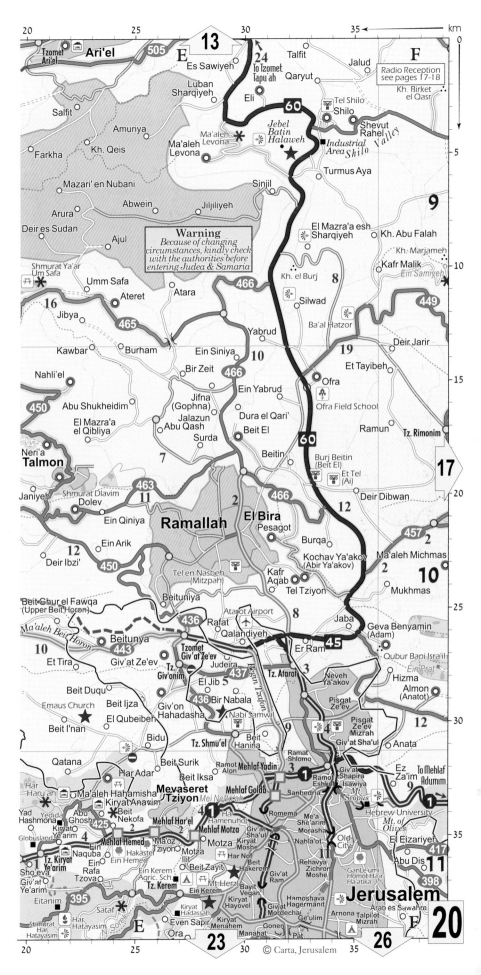

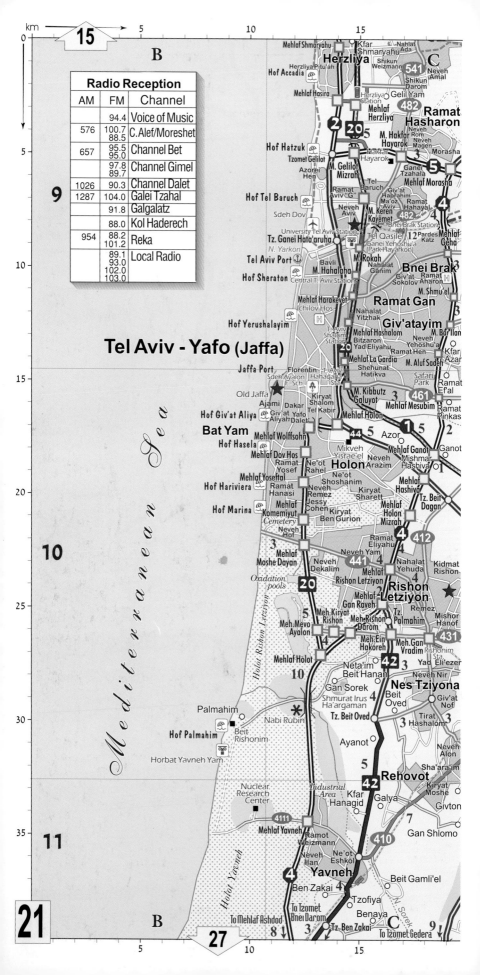

Radio Reception

AM	FM	Channel
	94.4	Voice of Music
576	100.7 / 88.5	C.Alef/Moreshet
657	95.5 / 95.0	Channel Bet
	97.8 / 89.7	Channel Gimel
1026	90.3	Channel Dalet
1287	104.0	Galei Tzahal
	91.8	Galgalatz
	88.0	Kol Haderech
954	88.2 / 101.2	Reka
	89.1 / 93.0 / 102.0 / 103.0	Local Radio

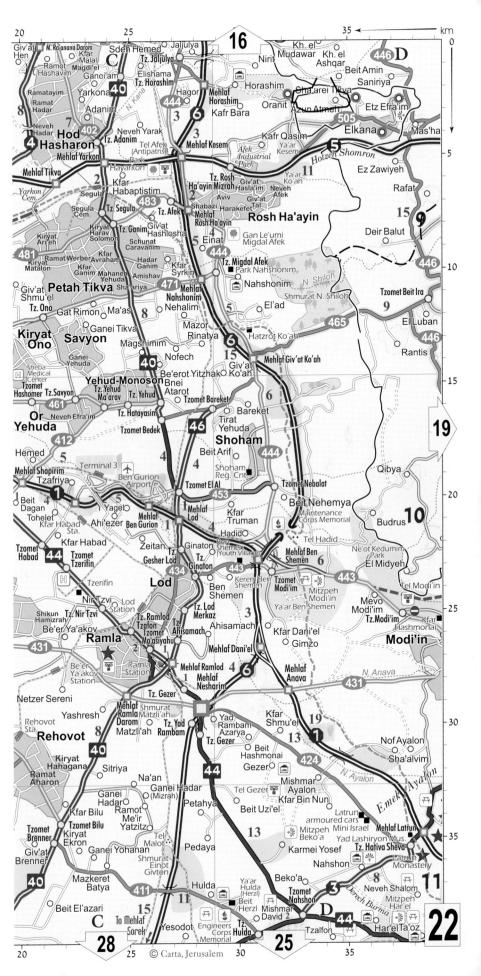

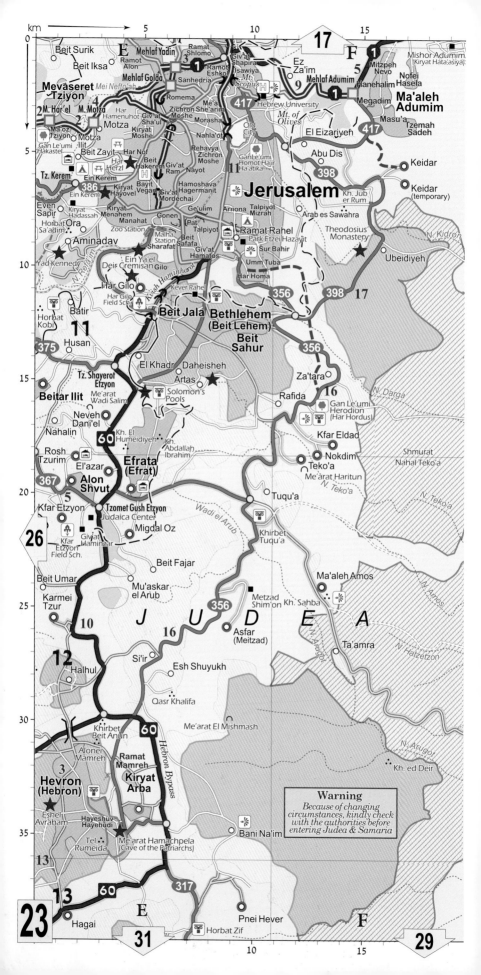

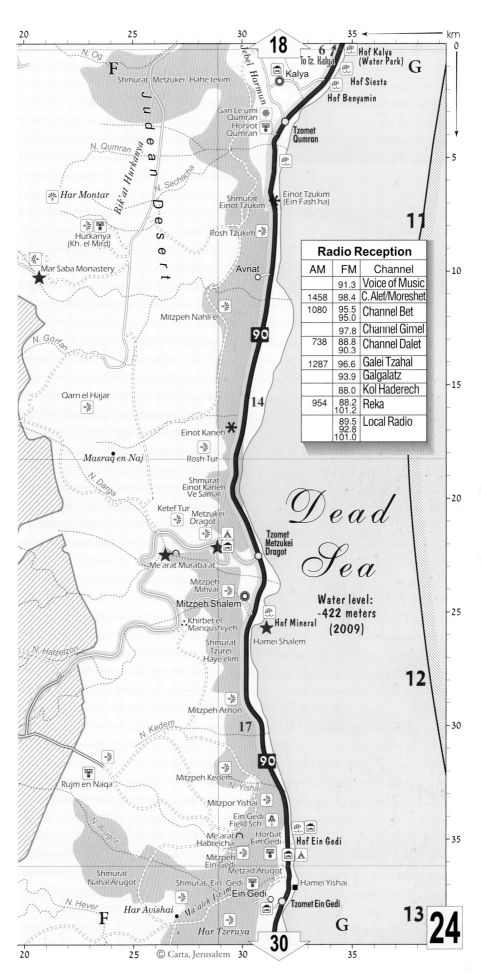

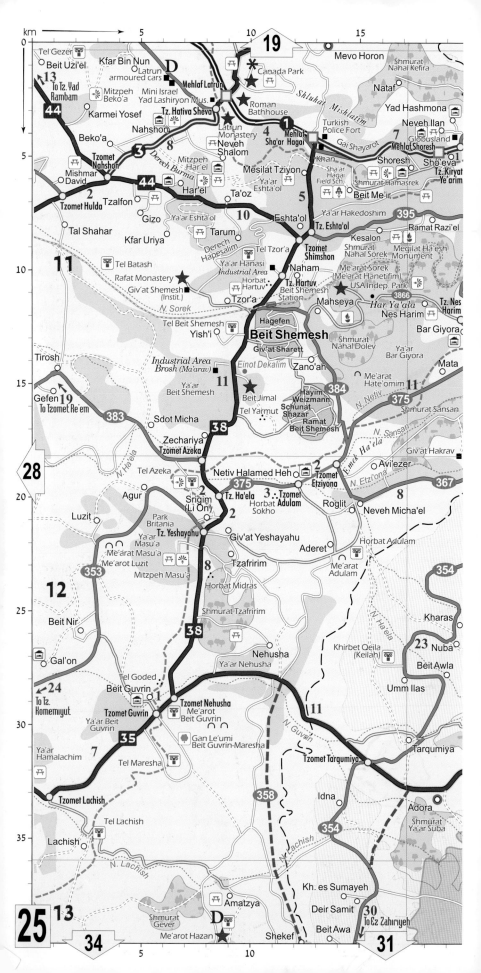

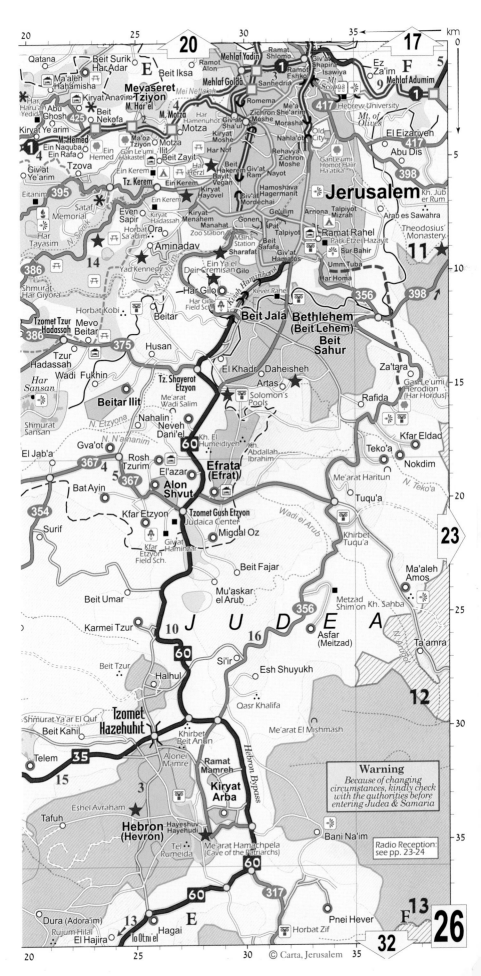

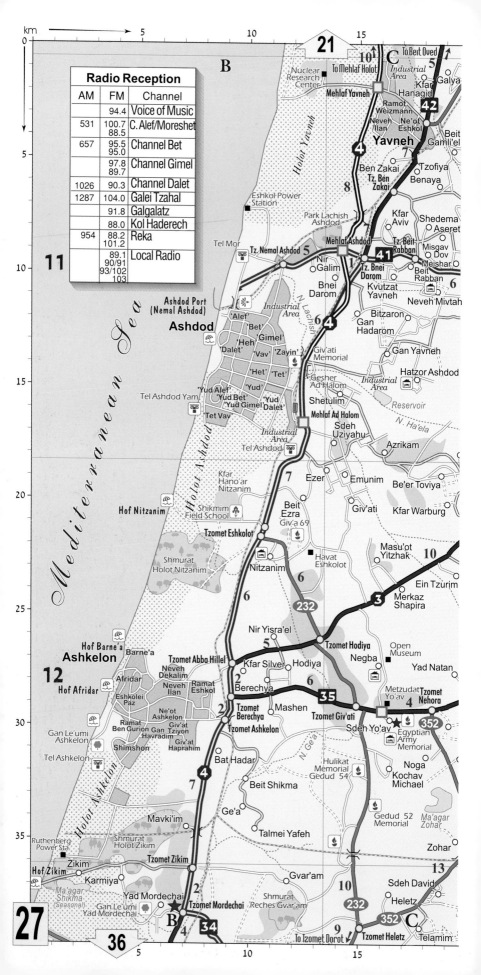

km
0   5   10   15

B

To Beit Oved

To Mehlaf Holot
To Mehlaf Holot

C

Industrial Area

Nuclear Research Center

Mehlaf Yavneh

Kfar Hanagid

Galya

Ramot Weizmann

Neveh Ilan

Ne'ot Eshkol

42

Radio Reception

AM	FM	Channel
	94.4	Voice of Music
531	100.7 88.5	C. Alef/Moreshet
657	95.5 95.0	Channel Bet
	97.8 89.7	Channel Gimel
1026	90.3	Channel Dalet
1287	104.0	Galei Tzahal
	91.8	Galgalatz
	88.0	Kol Haderech
954	88.2 101.2	Reka
	89.1 90/91 93/102 103	Local Radio

Yavneh

Holot Yavneh

Beit Gamli'el

Ben Zakai

Tz. Ben Zakai

Tzofiya

Benaya

4

8

Eshkol Power Station

Park Lachish Ashdod

Kfar Aviv

Shedema Aseret

Misgav Dov

11

Tel Mor

Tz. Nemal Ashdod

Mehlaf Ashdod

Tz. Beit Rabban

41

Nir Galim

Tz. Bnei Darom

Beit Rabban

Meishar

Bnei Darom

Kvutzat Yavneh

Neveh Mivtah

6

Mediterranean Sea

Ashdod Port (Nemal Ashdod)

Industrial Area

'Alef'

'Bet'

'Gimel'

'Heh'

'Dalet'

'Vav'

'Zayin'

6

4

Bitzaron

Gan Hadarom

Gan Yavneh

Ashdod

Giv'ati Memorial

Hatzor Ashdod

'Het'

'Tet'

Industrial Area

Reservoir

'Yud Alef'

'Yud Bet'

'Yud'

'Yud Gimel'

'Yud Dalet'

Gesher Ad Halom

Tel Ashdod Yam

'Tet Vav'

Shetulim

Mehlaf Ad Halom

Sdeh Uziyahu

N. Ha'ela

Industrial Area

Tel Ashdod

Azrikam

7

Ezer

Emunim

Be'er Toviya

Kfar Hano'ar Nitzanim

Hof Nitzanim

Beit Ezra

Giv'ati

Kfar Warburg

Shikmim Field School

Giv'a 69

Tzomet Eshkolot

Masu'ot Yitzhak

10

Shmurat Holot Nitzanim

Nitzanim

Havat Eshkolot

6

Ein Tzurim

Merkaz Shapira

6

232

3

Nir Yisra'el

Tzomet Hodiya

Open Museum

Hof Barne'a

Barne'a

5

Negba

Yad Natan

Ashkelon

Tzomet Abba Hillel

Kfar Silver

Hodiya

12

Hof Afridar

Afridar

Neveh Dekalim

Neveh Ilan

Ramat Eshkol

2

Berechya

6

Metzudat Yo'av

Tzomet Nehora

Eshkolei Paz

Ne'ot Ashkelon

Mashen

35

4

Gan Le'umi Ashkelon

Ramat Ben Gurion

Giv'at Havradim

Gan Tziyon

2

Tzomet Berechya

Tzomet Giv'ati

Sdeh Yo'av

352

Tel Ashkelon

Shimshon

Giv'at Haprahim

Tzomet Ashkelon

Egyptian Army Memorial

Noga

Bat Hadar

N. Ge'a

Kochav Michael

7

4

Beit Shikma

Hulikat Memorial Gedud 54

Ma'agar Zohar

Mavki'im

Ge'a

Talmei Yafeh

Gedud 52 Memorial

35

Holot Ashkelon

Ruthenberg Power Sta.

Shmurat Holot Zikim

Tzomet Zikim

Zohar

Hof Zikim

Zikim

Gvar'am

Sdeh David

13

Karmiya

Ma'agar Shikma (Seasonal)

2

10

232

Heletz

Yad Mordechai

Tzomet Mordechai

Shmurat Reches Gvar'am

352

C

Gan Le'umi Yad Mordechai

B

9

Telamim

27

4

34

To Tzomet Dorot

Tzomet Heletz

5   10   15

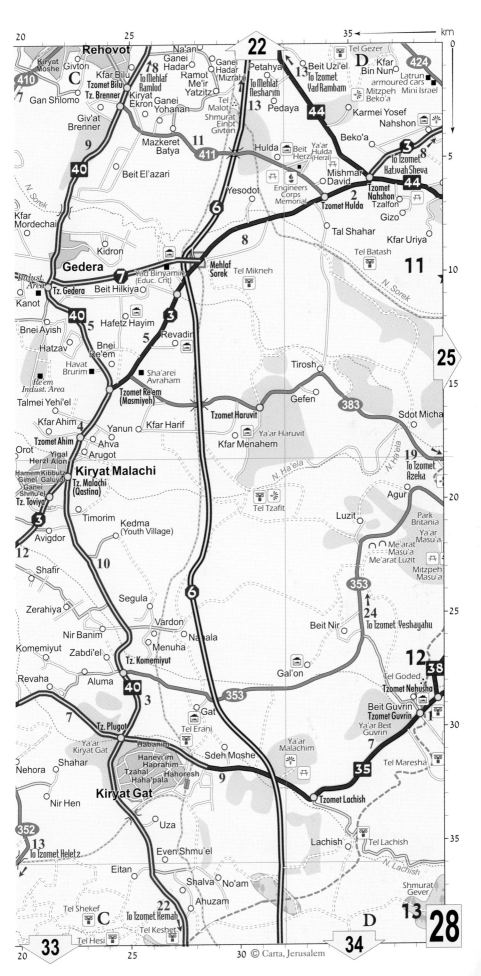

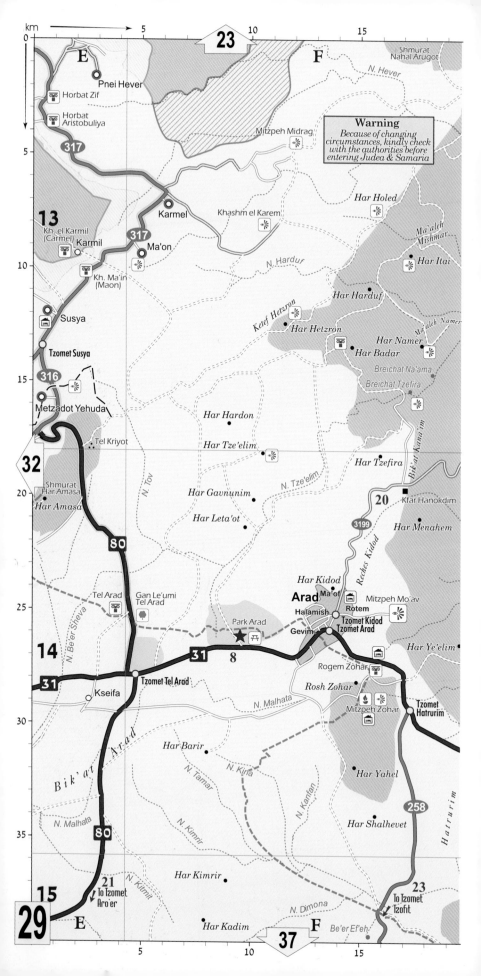

km →
0   5   10   15

23

E   F

Shmurat Nahal Arugot

Pnei Hever

Horbat Zif

Horbat Aristobuliya

Mitzpeh Midrag

Warning
Because of changing circumstances, kindly check with the authorities before entering Judea & Samaria

317

Har Holed

13

Karmel

Khashm el Karem

Ma`aleh Mishmar

Kh. el Karmil (Carmel)
Karmil

317

Ma'on

Har Itai

Kh. Ma'in (Maon)

N. Harduf

Har Harduf

Susya

Ketef Hetzron

Har Hetzron

Har Namer

Ma`aleh Namer

Tzomet Susya

Har Badar

316

Breichat Na'ama

Metzadot Yehuda

Breichat Tzefira

32

Tel Kriyot

Har Hardon

N. Tov

Har Tze'elim

Har Tzefira

Bik'at Kana'im

Shmurat Har Amasa

Har Gavnunim

N. Tze'elim

20

Har Amasa

Kfar Hanokdim

80

Har Leta'ot

3199

Har MenaS ham

Tel Arad

Gan Le'umi Tel Arad

Rechas Kidod

Har Kidod

Park Arad

Arad
Ma'of

Mitzpeh Mo'av

Halamish
Rotem

Har Ye'elim

14

31

8

Gevim
Tzomet Kidod
Tzomet Arad

Rogem Zohar

N. Be'er Sheva

Tzomet Tel Arad

Rosh Zohar

Tzomet Hatrurim

Kseifa

N. Malhata

Mitzpeh Zohar

Bik'at Arad

Har Barir

N. Kina

Har Yahel

N. Tamar

N. Kanfan

258

Hatrurim

N. Malhata

N. Kimrir

Har Shalhevet

80

15

21
To Tzomet Aro'er

Har Kimrir

23
To Tzomet Tzofit

29

E   N. Kitni   Har Kadim   N. Dimona   Be'er Ef'eh   **37**   F

5   10   15

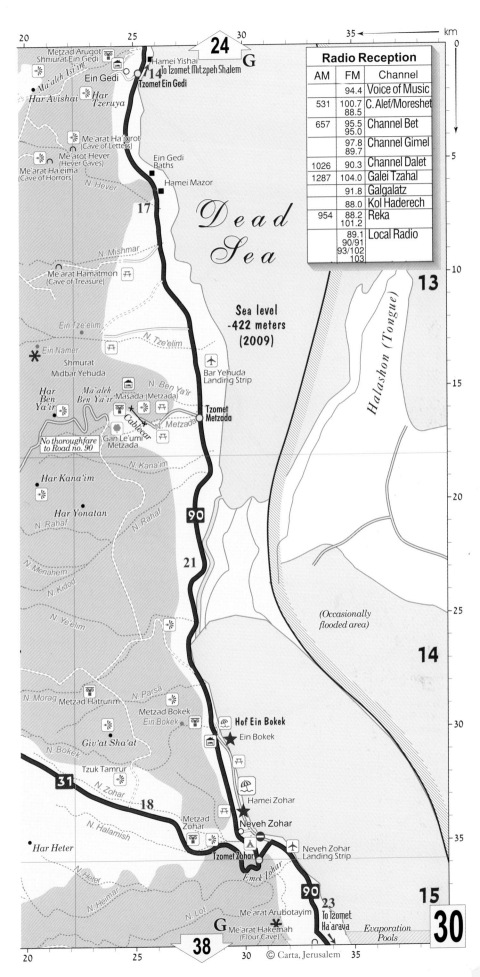

Radio Reception

AM	FM	Channel
	94.4	Voice of Music
531	100.7 / 88.5	C. Alef/Moreshet
657	95.5 / 95.0	Channel Bet
	97.8 / 89.7	Channel Gimel
1026	90.3	Channel Dalet
1287	104.0	Galei Tzahal
	91.8	Galgalatz
	88.0	Kol Haderech
954	88.2 / 101.2	Reka
	89.1 / 90/91 / 93/102 / 103	Local Radio

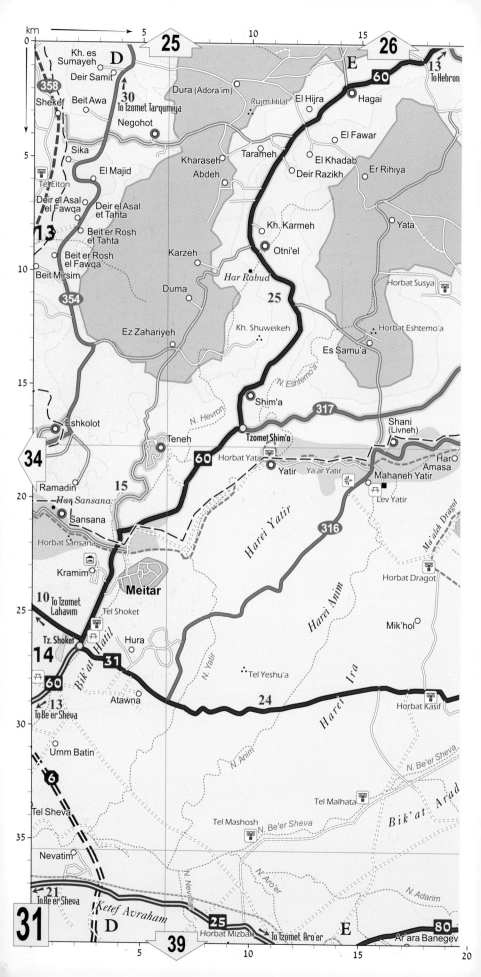

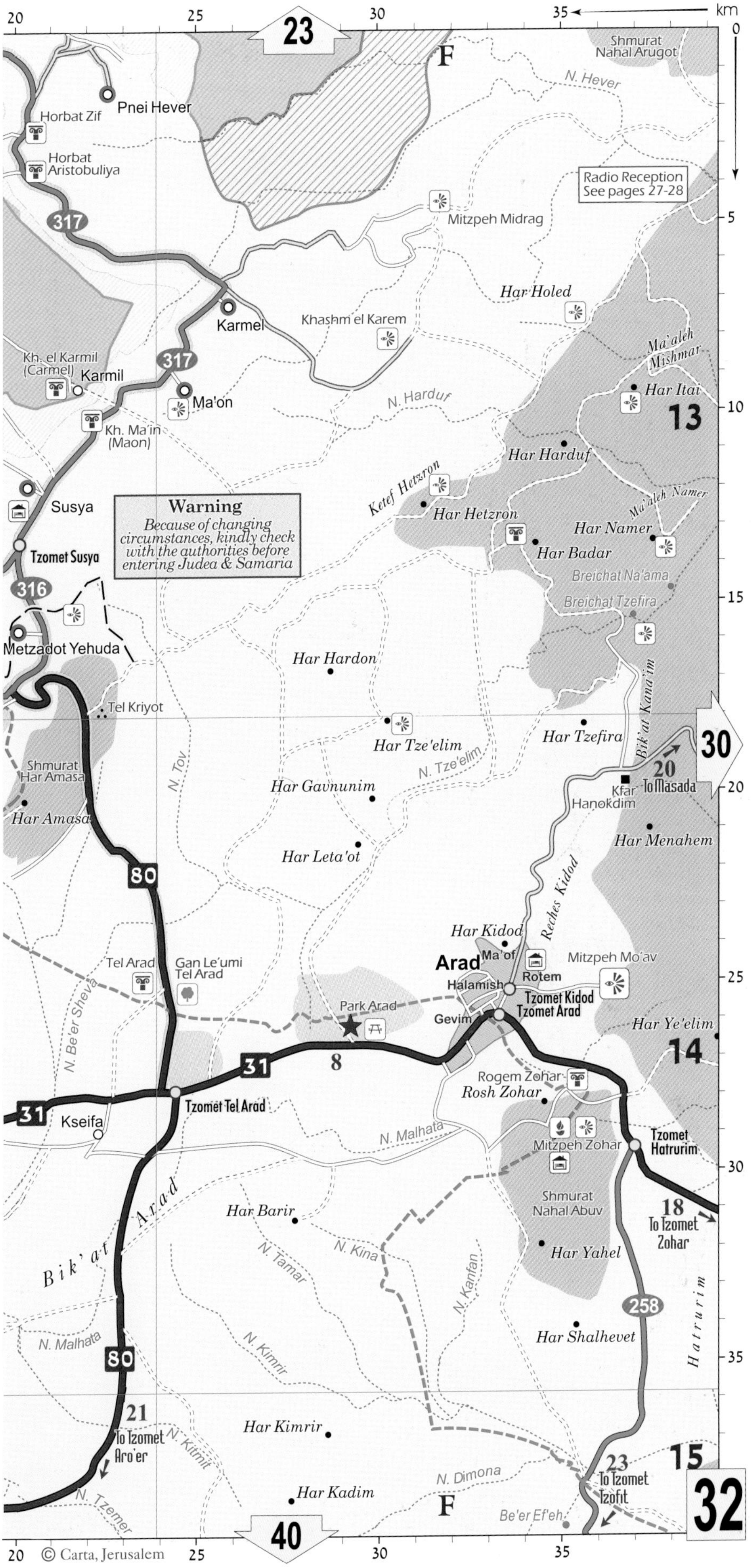

23
F
Shmurat Nahal Arugot
N. Hever
Pnei Hever
Horbat Zif
Horbat Aristobuliya
Radio Reception See pages 27-28
317
Mitzpeh Midrag
Har Holed
Karmel
Khashm el Karem
Ma'aleh Mishmar
Kh. el Karmil (Carmel)
Karmil
317
Ma'on
Har Itai
N. Harduf
13
Kh. Ma'in (Maon)
Har Harduf
Ketef Hetzron
Ma'aleh Namer
Susya
Har Hetzron
Warning
Because of changing circumstances, kindly check with the authorities before entering Judea & Samaria
Har Namer
Har Badar
Tzomet Susya
Breichat Na'ama
316
Breichat Tzefira
Metzadot Yehuda
Har Hardon
Tel Kriyot
Har Tze'elim
Har Tzefira
Bik'at Kana'im
30
Shmurat Har Amasa
N. Tov
N. Tze'elim
20
Har Gavnunim
Kfar Hanokdim
To Masada
Har Amasa
Har Menahem
Har Leta'ot
80
Reches Kidod
Har Kidod
Arad
Ma'of
Mitzpeh Mo'av
Tel Arad
Gan Le'umi Tel Arad
Rotem
Halamish
Tzomet Kidod
Park Arad
Tzomet Arad
Gevim
Har Ye'elim
N. Be'er Sheva
31
8
14
Rogem Zohar
Rosh Zohar
31
Tzomet Tel Arad
Kseifa
Mitzpeh Zohar
N. Malhata
Tzomet Hatrurim
Bik'at Arad
Shmurat Nahal Abuv
Har Barir
18
To Tzomet Zohar
N. Tamar
N. Kina
Har Yahel
N. Kanfan
258
Hatrurim
N. Malhata
N. Kimrir
Har Shalhevet
80
21
To Tzomet Aro'er
N. Kitmit
Har Kimrir
15
23
To Tzomet Tzofit
N. Dimona
Har Kadim
F
N. Tzemer
Be'er Ef'eh
40
32
20
25
30
35
km
0
5
10
15
20
25
30
35

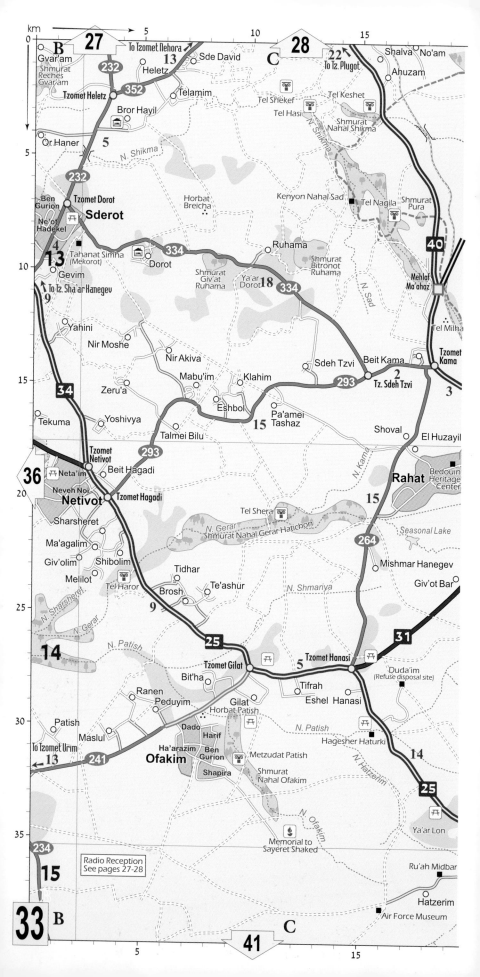

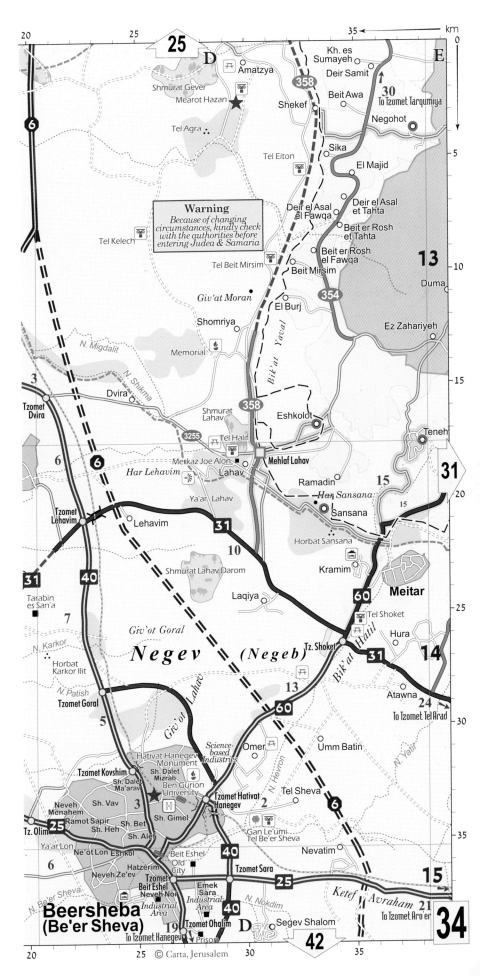

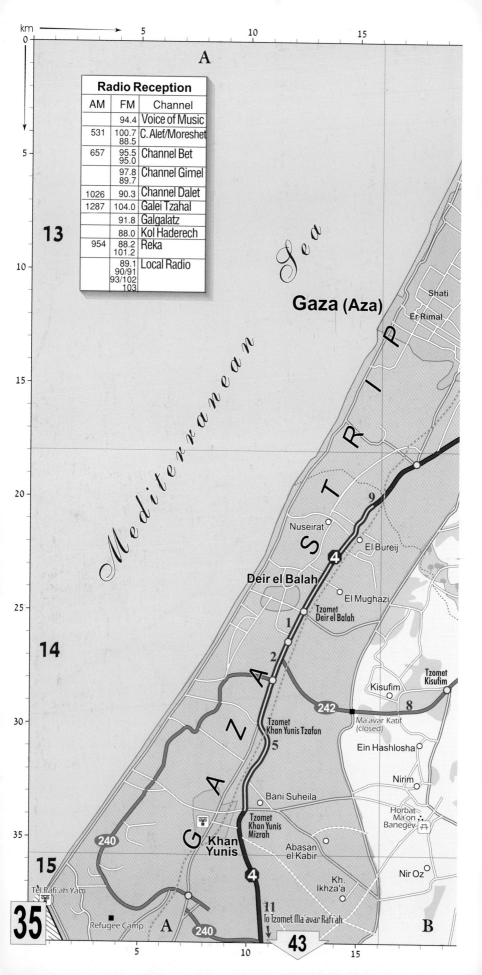

km

A

13

14

15

35

Radio Reception		
AM	FM	Channel
	94.4	Voice of Music
531	100.7 88.5	C. Alef/Moreshet
657	95.5 95.0	Channel Bet
	97.8 89.7	Channel Gimel
1026	90.3	Channel Dalet
1287	104.0	Galei Tzahal
	91.8	Galgalatz
	88.0	Kol Haderech
954	88.2 101.2	Reka
	89.1 90/91 93/102 103	Local Radio

Mediterranean Sea

Gaza (Aza)

Shati

Er Rimal

S T R I P

9

Nuseirat

El Bureij

4

Deir el Balah

El Mughazi

Tzomet
Deir el Balah

1

2

Kisufim

Tzomet
Kisufim

242

8

Ma'avar Katif
(closed)

Tzomet
Khan Yunis Tzafon

5

Ein Hashlosha

Nirim

Bani Suheila

Horbat
Ma'on
Banegev

G A Z A

Tzomet
Khan Yunis
Mizrah

240

**Khan
Yunis**

Abasan
el Kabir

Nir Oz

Kh.
Ikhza'a

4

Tel Rafi'ah Yam

11
To Tzomet Ma'avar Rafi'ah

Refugee Camp

A

240

43

B

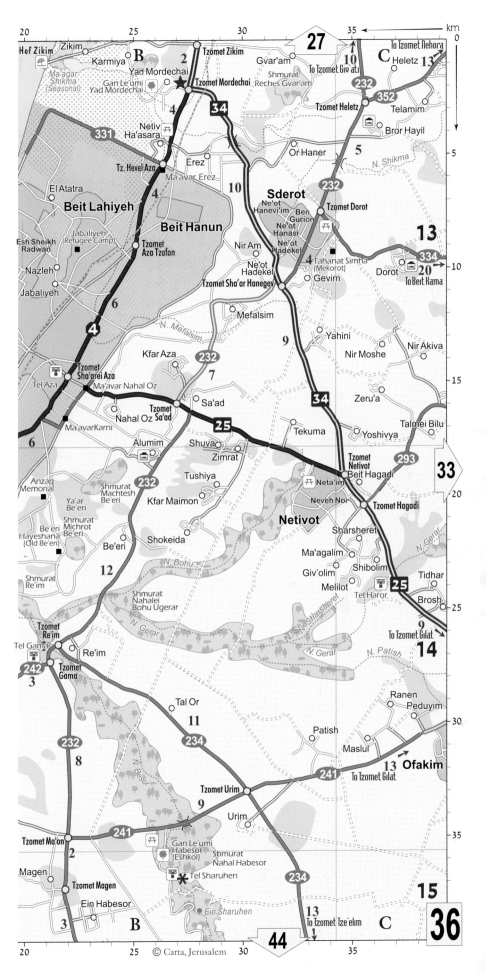

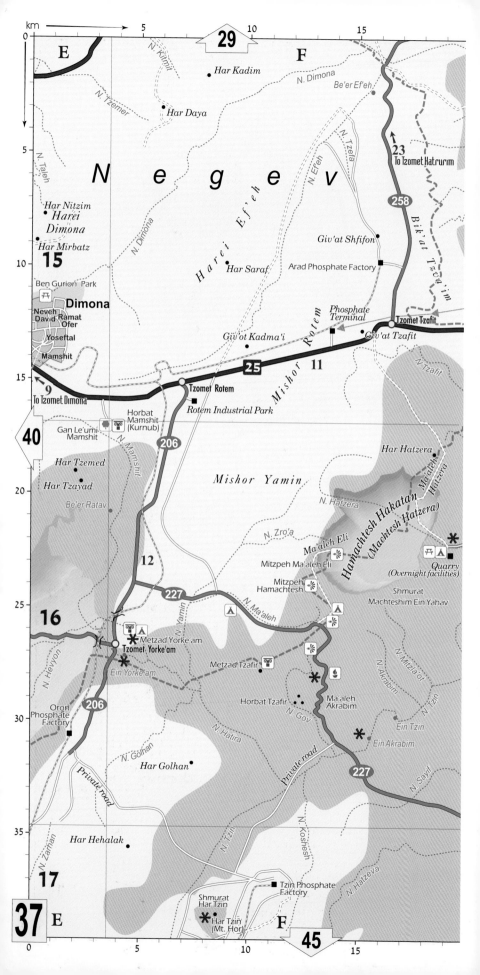

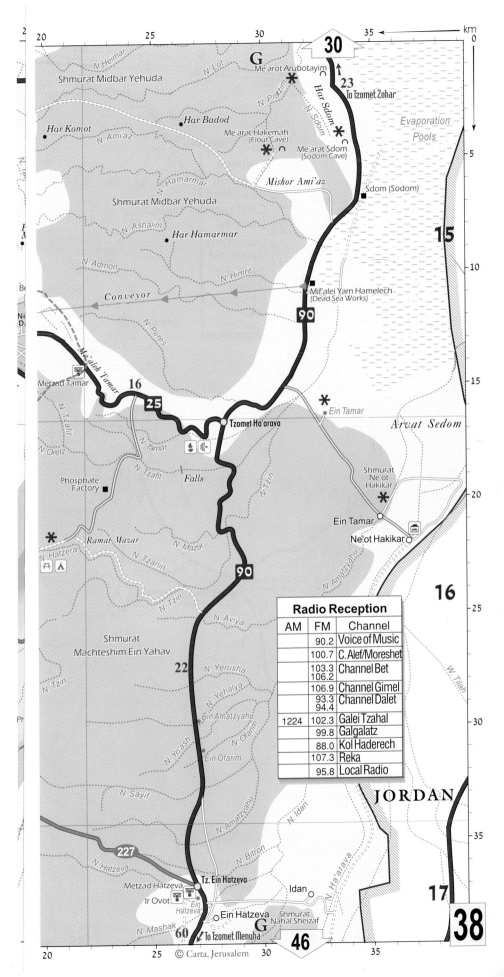

km

23
To Tzomet Zohar

G
Me'arot Arubotayim

Har Sdom

Evaporation Pools

Shmurat Midbar Yehuda

Har Komot

Har Badod

N. Heimar

N. Lot

N. Prazim

N. Sdom

Me'arat Hakemah
(Flour Cave)

Me'arat Sdom
(Sodom Cave)

Sdom (Sodom)

N. Ami'az

15

5

Mishor Ami'az

Shmurat Midbar Yehuda

N. Hamarmar

Har Hamarmar

N. Ashalim

N. Admon

N. Himrit

10

Conveyor

N. Peres

Mif'alei Yam Hamelech
(Dead Sea Works)

90

Ma'aleh Tamar

Metzad Tamar

N. Tzafit

16

25

Tzomet Ha'arava

Ein Tamar

Arvat Sedom

15

N. Tamar

Falls

N. Tzin

Phosphate
Factory

N. Oretz

Shmurat Ne'ot
Hakikar

20

Ein Tamar

Ne'ot Hakikar

Ramat Mazar

N. Hatzera

N. Mazar

N. Tzanin

N. Amatzyahu

W. Tilah

90

Shmurat
Machteshim Ein Yahav

N. Tzin

22

N. Aviya

N. Yerusha

N. Yehalya

Ein Amatzyahu

N. Ofarim

Ein Ofarim

N. Yo'ash

16

25

Radio Reception		
AM	**FM**	**Channel**
	90.2	Voice of Music
	100.7	C. Alef/Moreshet
	103.3 106.2	Channel Bet
	106.9	Channel Gimel
	93.3 94.4	Channel Dalet
1224	102.3	Galei Tzahal
	99.8	Galgalatz
	88.0	Kol Haderech
	107.3	Reka
	95.8	Local Radio

J O R D A N

N. Sayif

N. Idan

30

N. Amatzyahu

35

N. Bitron

N. Ha'arava

227

N. Hatzeva

Tz. Ein Hatzeva

Metzad Hatzeva

Idan

Ir Ovot

Ein
Hatzeva

Ein Hatzeva

Shmurat
Nahal Sheizaf

17

N. Mashak

60
To Tzomet Menuha

G

46

© Carta, Jerusalem

38

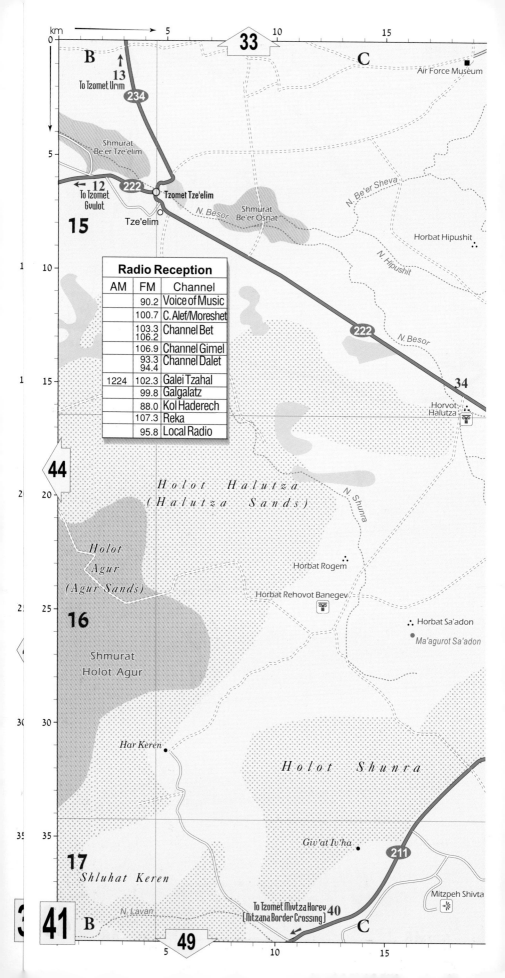

Radio Reception		
AM	FM	Channel
	90.2	Voice of Music
	100.7	C. Alef/Moreshet
	103.3 106.2	Channel Bet
	106.9	Channel Gimel
	93.3 94.4	Channel Dalet
1224	102.3	Galei Tzahal
	99.8	Galgalatz
	88.0	Kol Haderech
	107.3	Reka
	95.8	Local Radio

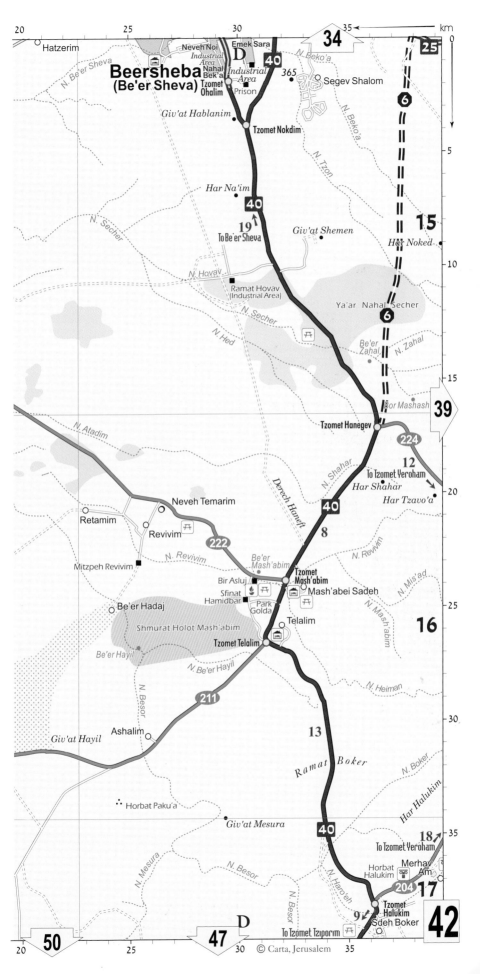

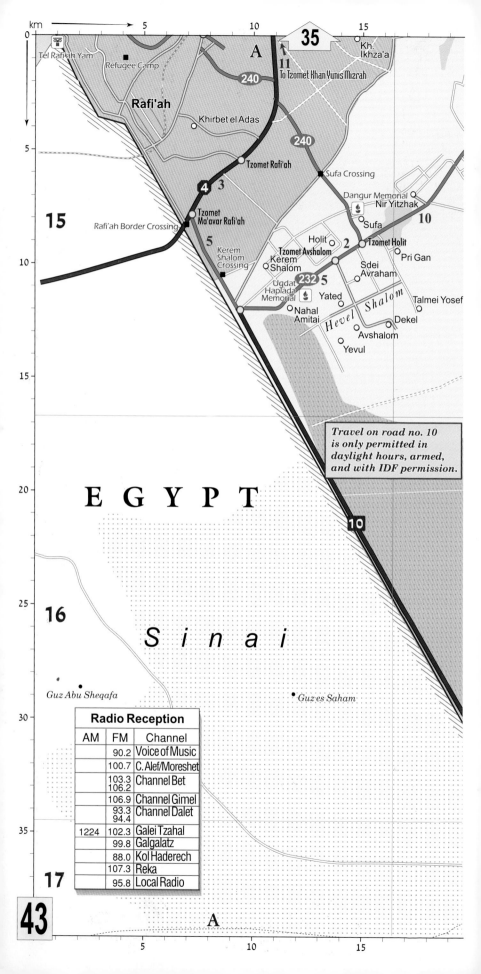

km

35

A

To Tzomet Khan Yunis Mizrah

240

Tel Rafi'ah Yam

Refugee Camp

Rafi'ah

Khirbet el Adas

240

Kh. Ikhza'a

Tzomet Rafi'ah

Sufa Crossing

15

4 3

Dangur Memorial

Nir Yitzhak

Tzomet
Ma'avar Rafi'ah

Sufa

10

Rafi'ah Border Crossing

5

Holit

2 Tzomet Holit

Kerem
Shalom
Crossing

Tzomet Avshalom

Pri Gan

Kerem
Shalom

232 5

Sdei
Avraham

Ugdat
Haplada
Memorial

Yated

Talmei Yosef

Nahal
Amitai

Hevel Shalom

Dekel

Avshalom

Yevul

E G Y P T

*Travel on road no. 10
is only permitted in
daylight hours, armed,
and with IDF permission.*

10

16

S i n a i

Guz Abu Sheqafa

Guz es Saham

Radio Reception		
AM	FM	Channel
	90.2	Voice of Music
	100.7	C. Alef/Moreshet
	103.3 106.2	Channel Bet
	106.9	Channel Gimel
	93.3 94.4	Channel Dalet
1224	102.3	Galei Tzahal
	99.8	Galgalatz
	88.0	Kol Haderech
	107.3	Reka
	95.8	Local Radio

17

43

A

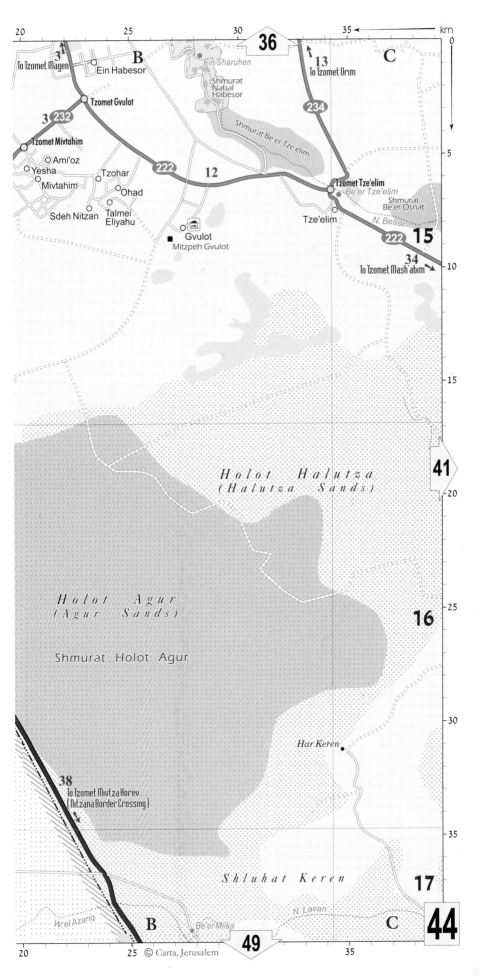

km

B

C

3¹
To Tzomet Magen

Ein Habesor

Ein Sharuhen

Shmurat
Nahal Habesor

13
To Tzomet Urim

Tzomet Gvulot

234

3 232

Shmurat Be'er Tze'elim

Tzomet Mivtahim

Ami'oz

222

12

Yesha

Tzohar

Mivtahim

Ohad

Tzomet Tze'elim
Be'er Tze'elim

Shmurat
Be'er Osnat

Sdeh Nitzan

Talmei
Eliyahu

Tze'elim

N. Besor

222

15

Gvulot
Mitzpeh Gvulot

34
To Tzomet Mash'abim

Holot Halutza
(Halutza Sands)

41

Holot Agur
(Agur Sands)

16

Shmurat Holot Agur

Har Keren

38
To Tzomet Mivtza Horev
(Nitzana Border Crossing)

Shluhat Keren

17

W. el Azariq

B

Be'er Milka

N. Lavan

C

44

© Carta, Jerusalem

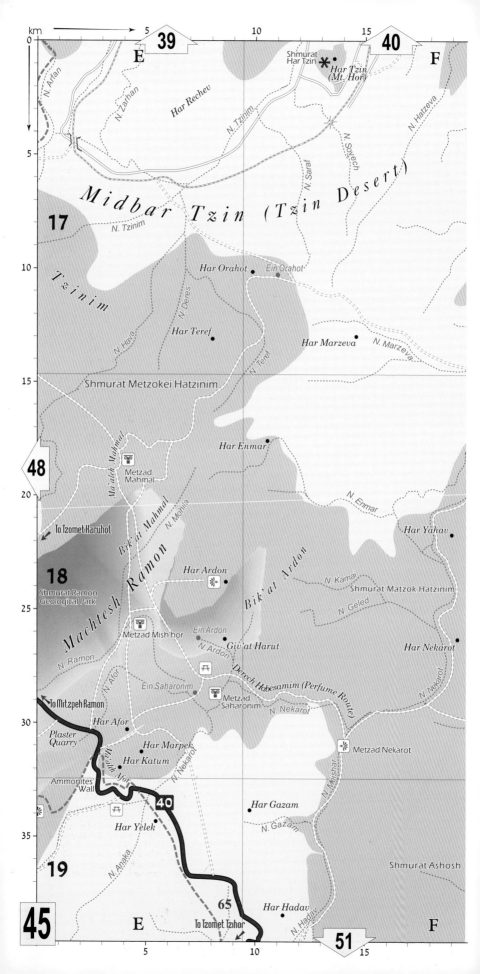

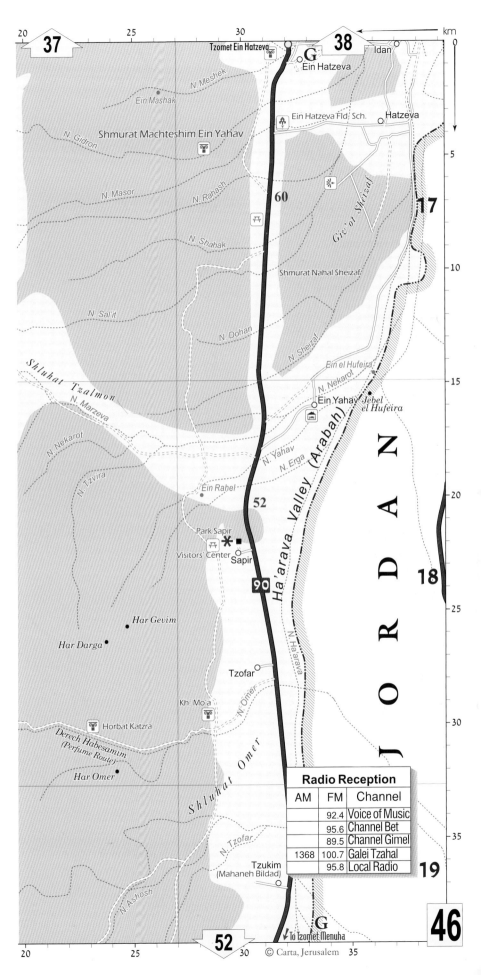

37

38

km

Tzomet Ein Hatzeva

G

Ein Hatzeva

Idan

N. Meshek

Ein Mashak

Ein Hatzeva Fld. Sch.

Hatzeva

Shmurat Machteshim Ein Yahav

N. Gidron

60

Giv'ot Sheizaf

17

N. Masor

N. Rahash

N. Shahak

Shmurat Nahal Sheizaf

N. Sal'it

N. Dohan

N. Sheizaf

Ein el Hufeira

Shluhat Tzalmon

N. Nekarot

N. Marzeva

Ein Yahav

Jebel el Hufeira

N. Nekarot

N. Yahav

N. Erga

N. Tzvira

Ein Rahel

52

Park Sapir

Visitors' Center

Sapir

90

J O R D A N

18

Har Gevim

Ha'arava Valley (Arabah)

Har Darga

Tzofar

N. Ha'arava

Kh. Mo'a

N. Omer

Derech Habesamim (Perfume Route)

Horbat Katzra

Har Omer

Shluhat Omer

Radio Reception		
AM	FM	Channel
	92.4	Voice of Music
	95.6	Channel Bet
	89.5	Channel Gimel
1368	100.7	Galei Tzahal
	95.8	Local Radio

N. Tzofar

Tzukim (Mahaneh Bildad)

19

N. Ashosh

G

→ To Tzomet Menuha

52

© Carta, Jerusalem

46

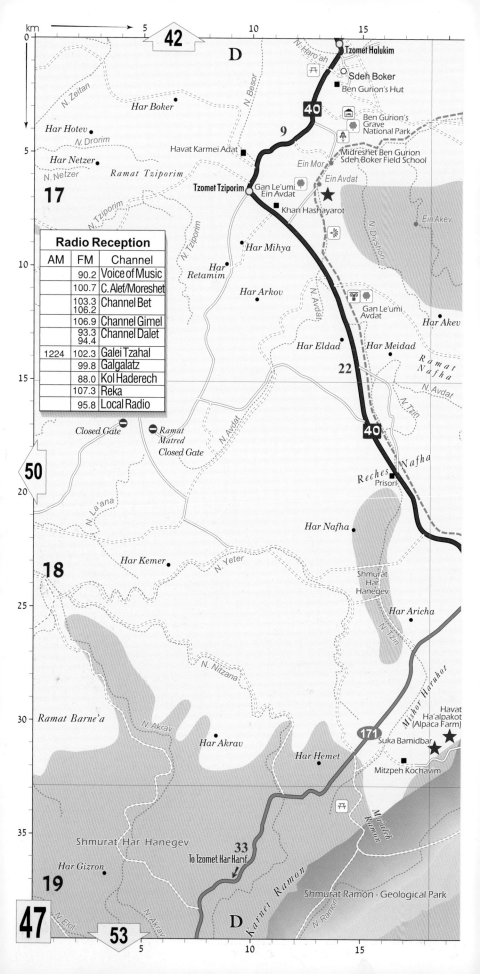

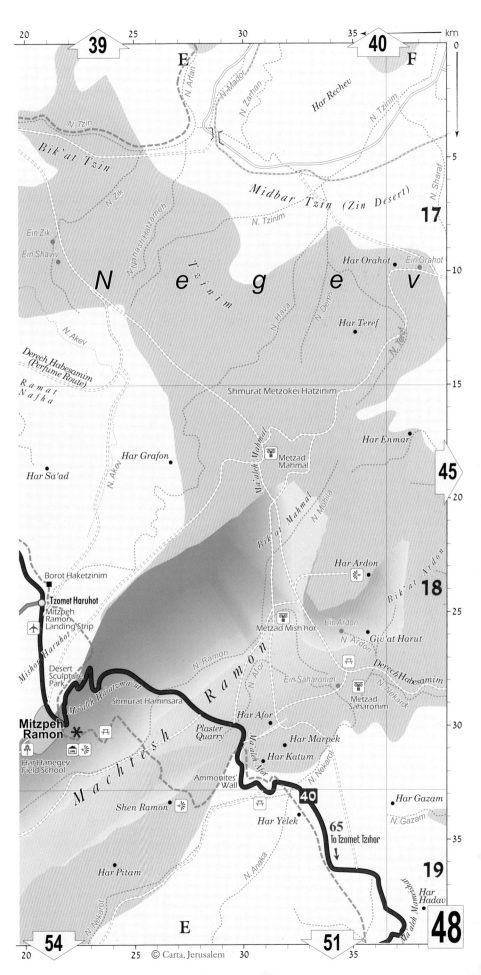

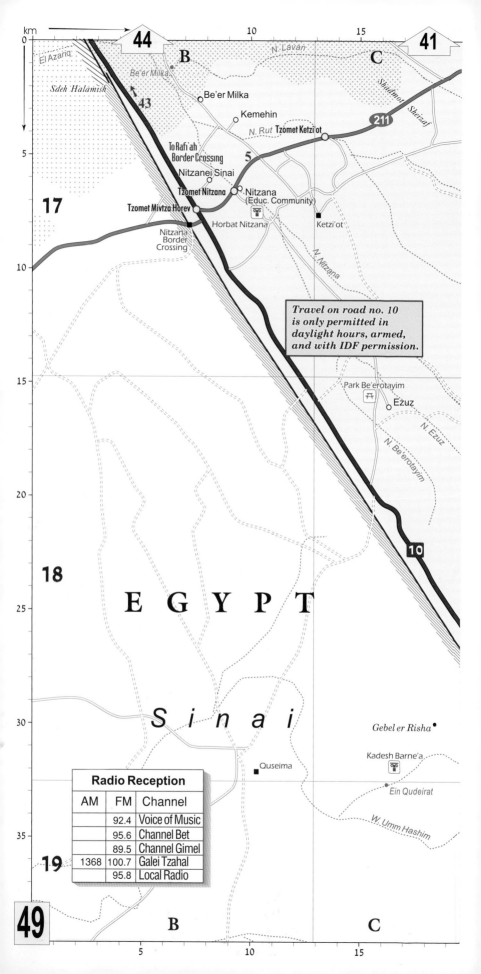

km

44   B   N. Lavan   C   41

El Azariq

Be'er Milka

Sdeh Halamish

43

Be'er Milka

Kemehin   N. Rut   Tzomet Ketzi'ot

211

To Rafi'ah
Border Crossing   5

Nitzanei Sinai

Tzomet Nitzana   Nitzana
                      (Educ. Community)
Tzomet Mivtza Horev

Shadmot Shetzaf

17   Horbat Nitzana   Ketzi'ot

Nitzana
Border
Crossing   N. Nitzana

Travel on road no. 10
is only permitted in
daylight hours, armed,
and with IDF permission.

Park Be'erotayim

Ezuz

N. Be'erotayim   N. Ezuz

10

18   E G Y P T

Gebel er Risha

Kadesh Barne'a

S i n a i

Quseima   Ein Qudeirat

W. Umm Hashim

Radio Reception		
AM	FM	Channel
	92.4	Voice of Music
	95.6	Channel Bet
	89.5	Channel Gimel
1368	100.7	Galei Tzahal
	95.8	Local Radio

19

49   B   10   C   15

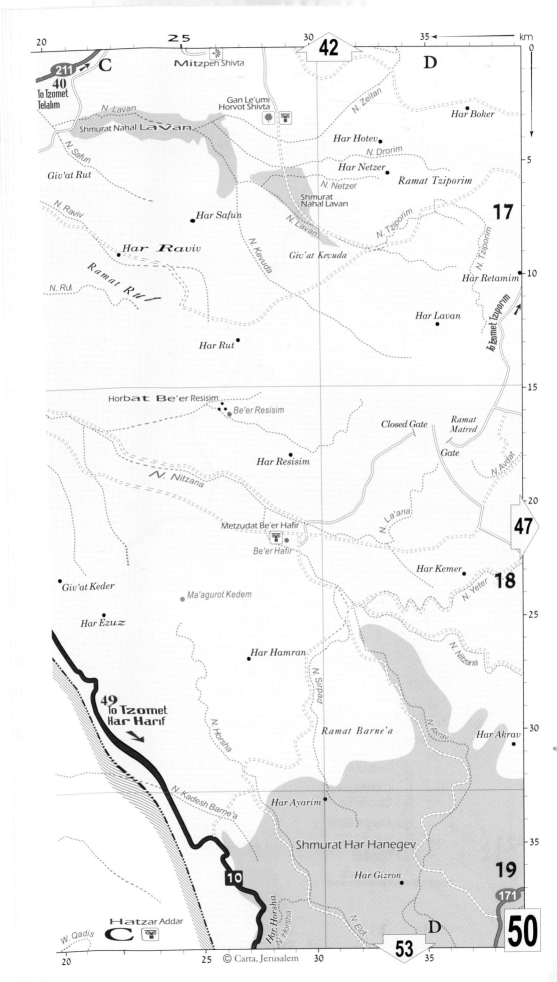

211 C
40
To Tzomet
Telalim

Mitzpeh Shivta

Gan Le'umi
Horvot Shivta

D

N. Zeitan

Har Boker

N. Lavan

Shmurat Nahal *Lavan*

N. Safun

Giv'at Rut

Har Hotev

N. Drorim

Har Netzer

N. Netzer

Ramat Tziporim

Shmurat
Nahal Lavan

Har Safun

N. Raviv

N. Lavan

Giv'at Kevuda

N. Tziporim

N. Tziporim

17

Har Retamim

Har *Raviv*

Ramat Ruf

N. Kevuda

To Tzomet Tziporim

N. Ruf

Har Lavan

Har Rut

Horbat Be'er Resisim

Be'er Resisim

Closed Gate

Ramat
Matred

Gate

N. Avdat

Har Resisim

N. Nitzana

20

Metzudat Be'er Hafir

N. La'ana

47

Be'er Hafir

Har Kemer

N. Yeter

18

Giv'at Keder

Ma'agurot Kedem

25

Har Ezuz

Har Hamran

N. Nitzana

N. Horsha

N. Sirpad

49
To Tzomet
Har Harif

Ramat Barne'a

N. Akrav

Har Akrav

30

N. Kadesh Barne'a

Har Ayarim

Shmurat Har Hanegev

35

10

Har Gizron

19

171

Hatzar Addar
C

N. Horsha

Har Horsha

N. Elot

D

50

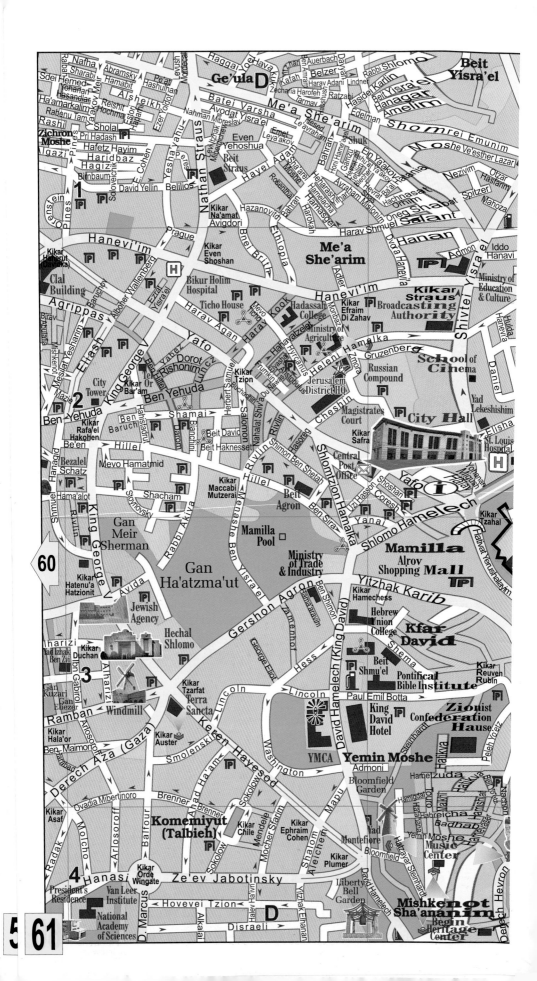

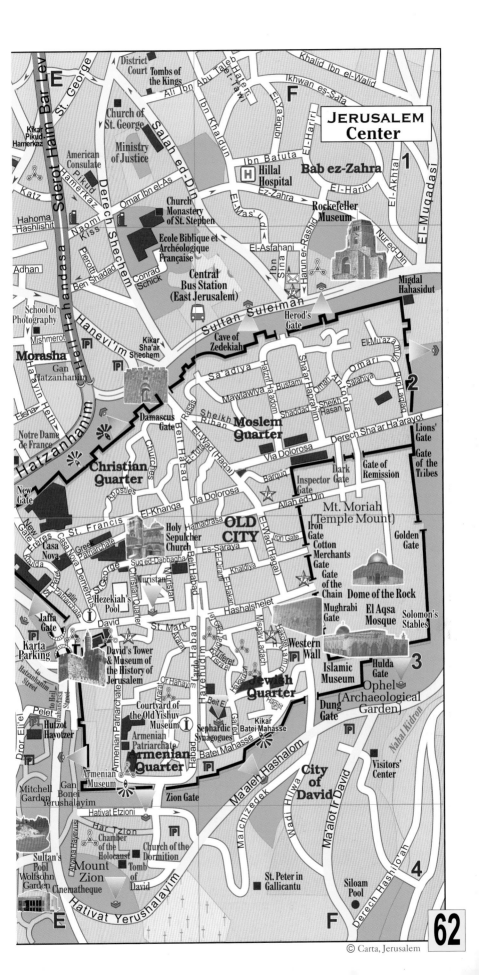

JERUSALEM
Center

E

District Court
Tombs of the Kings
Church of St. George
American Consulate
Ministry of Justice
Kikar Pikud Hamerkaz
Salah ed-Din
Omar Ibn el-As
Derech Shechem
Pikud Hamerkaz
Hahoma Hashlishit
Katz
Naomi Kiss
Adhan
Pierotti
Ben Shaddad
Conrad Schick
Church Monastery of St. Stephen
Ecole Biblique et Archéologique Française
School of Photography
Mishmerot
Hanevi'im
Kikar Sha'ar Shechem
Central Bus Station (East Jerusalem)
Morasha
Gan Hatzanhanim
Hahandasa
Ha'ayin Heth
Hahandasa
Elisha
Hatzanhanim
Damascus Gate
Notre Dame de France
Churches
Rashi
Beit Ha'Lad
Christian Quarter
New Gate
New Gate
St. Francis
Frères
Casa Nova
Casa Nova
Greek Patriarchate
Greek Orthodox Demetrius
El-Khanga
Apostles
Via Dolorosa
Hamadrasa
Holy Sepulcher Church
OLD CITY
Casa Nova
Anuda
St. Peter
Latin Patriarchate
St. George
Christian Quarter
Muristan
Suq ed-Dabbagha
Muristan
Hezekiah's Pool
Beit Habad
Es-Saraya
El-Oram
Khaldiya
Mt. Moriah (Temple Mount)
Jaffa Gate
David
St. Mark
Ararat
Karta Parking
Hatzanhanim Street
to Hell
David's Tower & Museum of the History of Jerusalem
Afula
Or Hahayim
Cardo
Habad
Havehudim
Chain Tiferet
Beit El
Hashalshelet
Hakehuna
Misgav Ladach
Plugot HaKotel
Hagai
Tiferet Israel
Hashalshelet
Dror El'Ile
Hutzot Hayotzer
Pelet
Courtyard of the Old Yishuv Museum
Ararat
Habad
Gal Ed
Beit El
Jewish Quarter
Sephardic Synagogues
Kikar Batei Mahasse
Batei Mahasse
Armenian Patriarchate
Armenian Patriarchate
Armenian Museum
Armenian Quarter
Mitchell Garden
Gan Bonei Yerushalayim
Zion Gate
Malchizedek
Maaleh Hashalom
Sultan's Pool
Wolfsohn Garden
Cinematheque
Hativat Etzioni
Har Tzion
Ayana Hayerus
Chamber of the Holocaust
Church of the Dormition
Mount Zion
Tomb of David
Hativat Yerushalayim

F

Khalid Ibn el-Walid
Ali Ibn Abu Taleb
Hatem
Ibn Khaldun
El-Yaaqubi
Ikhwan es-Safa
El-Hariri
El-Akhtal
El-Muqadasi
Ibn Batuta
Bab ez-Zahra
Hillal Hospital H
Ez-Zahra
Rockefeller Museum
Harun er-Rashid
El-Mas'udi
Nured-Din
El-Asfahani
Ibn Sina
Migdal Hahasidut
El-Mu'azamia
Sultan Suleiman
Herod's Gate
Cave of Zedekiah
Sa'adiya
Hatzrit Ha'adom
Shaar Haprahim
Mawlawiya
Bustam
Omari
Aqabat
An Nabi
Shaddad
Sheikh Hasan
Salahia
Omari
Burj Laqlaq
Sheikh Rihan
Moslem Quarter
El-Wad (Hagai)
El-Wad (Hagai)
Via Dolorosa
Barquq
Via Dolorosa
Allah ed-Din
Derech Sha'ar Ha'arayot
Lions' Gate
Gate of the Tribes
Dark Gate
Gate of Remission
Inspector Gate
Iron Gate
Cotton Merchants Gate
Gate of the Chain
Golden Gate
Dome of the Rock
Mughrabi Gate
El Aqsa Mosque
Solomon's Stables
Western Wall
Hakotel Hama'aravi
Islamic Museum
Hulda Gate
Ophel (Archaeological Garden)
Dung Gate
City of David
Wadi Hilwa
Ma'alot Ir David
Visitors' Center
Nahal Kidron
St. Peter in Gallicantu
Siloam Pool
Derech Hashiloah

1

2

3

4

© Carta, Jerusalem

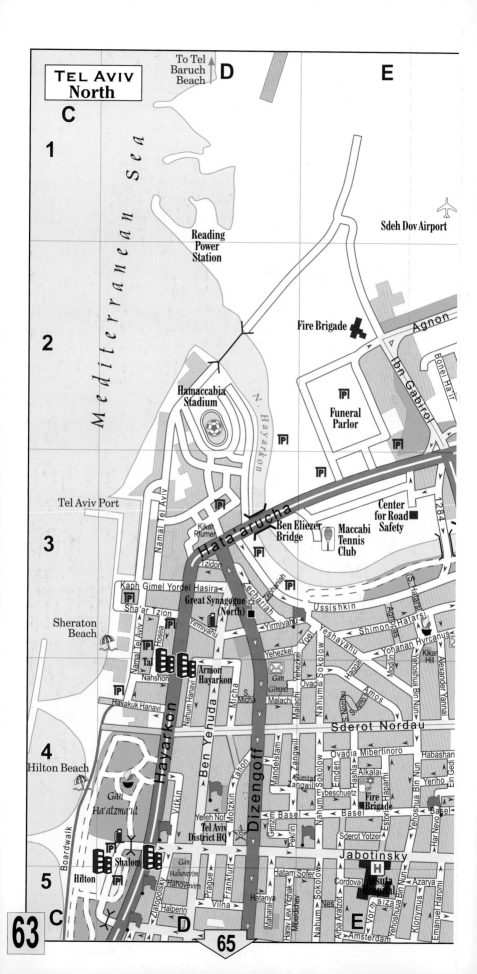

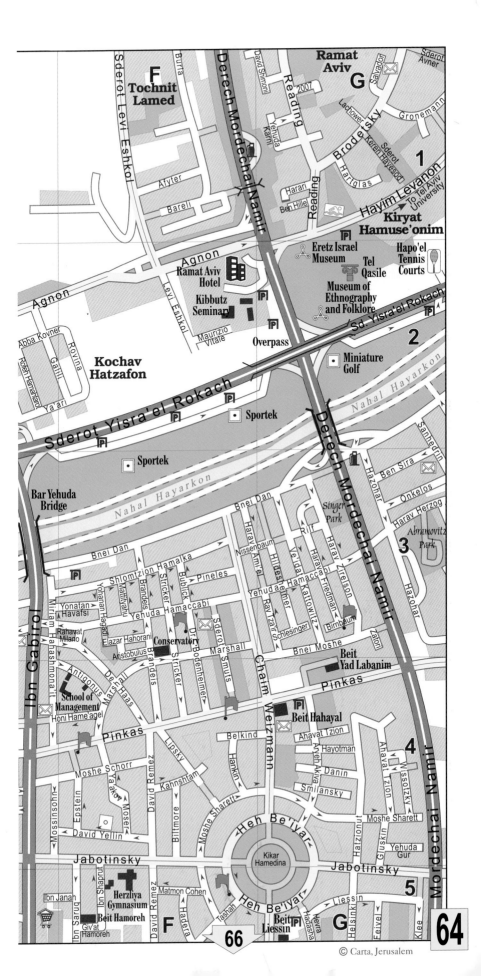

Tochnit Lamed

Ramat Aviv

F

G

Sderot Levi Eshkal

Burla

David Shimoni

Reading

2007

Salvador

Sderot Avner

Lachower

Brod etsky

Keren Hayesod

Sderot Gronemann

Afyter

Yehuda Karni

Brodetsky

Hartglas

1

Bareli

Harari

Reading

Ben Hillel

Hayim Levanon

To Tel Aviv University

Kiryat Hamuse'onim

Agnon

Ramat Aviv Hotel

Levi Eshkal

Eretz Israel Museum

Tel Qasile

Hapo'el Tennis Courts

Kibbutz Seminary

Museum of Ethnography and Folklore

Agnon

Abba Kovner

Rovina

Galili

Maurizio Vitale

Overpass

Sd. Yisra'el Rokach

2

Rolen Hamataror

Ya'ari

Kochav Hatzafon

Miniature Golf

Nahal Hayarkon

Sderot Yisra'el Rokach

Derech Mordechai Namir

Sanhedrin

Sportek

Sportek

Ben Sira

Onkelos

Hazorea

Bar Yehuda Bridge

Nahal Hayarkon

Bnei Dan

Singer Park

Harav Herzog

Abramovitz Park

Bnei Dan

Harav Amrei

Nissenbaum

Hildesheimer

Ye'ida Hamaccabi

Harari Friedman

Harav Zirelson

3

Hazorah

Ibn Gabirol

Shlomtzion Hamalka

Brandeis

Stricker

Bublick

Pineles

Yehuda Hamaccabi

Rav zair

Schlesinger

Birnbaum

Zaton

Miriam Hanashmona'it

Yonatan Havafsi

Yohanan Hagadi

Matityahu

Elazar Hahorani

Conservatory

Sderot Smuts

Dr. Bodenheimer

Marshall

Bnei Moshe

Beit Yad Labanim

Rahavat Milano

Atistobulus

Brandeis

Stricker

Pinkas

Antigonus

De La Haas

Marsh Haas

School of Management

Honi Hame'agel

Pinkas

Belkind

Chaim Weizmann

Beit Hahayal

Ahavat Tzion

Ahavat Tzion

4

Moshe Schorr

Lipsky

David Remez

Kahnshtam

Hankin

Hayotman

Aryeh Akiva

Danin

Wissozky

Mossinsohn

Epstein

Ya'akov Mosel

David Yellin

Biltmore

Moshe Sharett

Smilansky

Moshe Sharett

Hatzionut

Gluskin

Yehuda Gur

Jabotinsky

Jabotinsky

Mordechai Namir

Ibn Janah

Ibn Saruq

Ibn Shaprut

Herzliya Gymnasium

Beit Hamoreh

David Remez

Matmon Cohen

Hadera

Tashan

Heh Be'iyar

Kikar Hamedina

Heh Be'iyar

Beit Liessin

Liessin

Helsinki

Hevra Hadasha

Feivel

Klee

5

Giv'at Hamoreh

Hadera

F

66

G

64

© Carta, Jerusalem

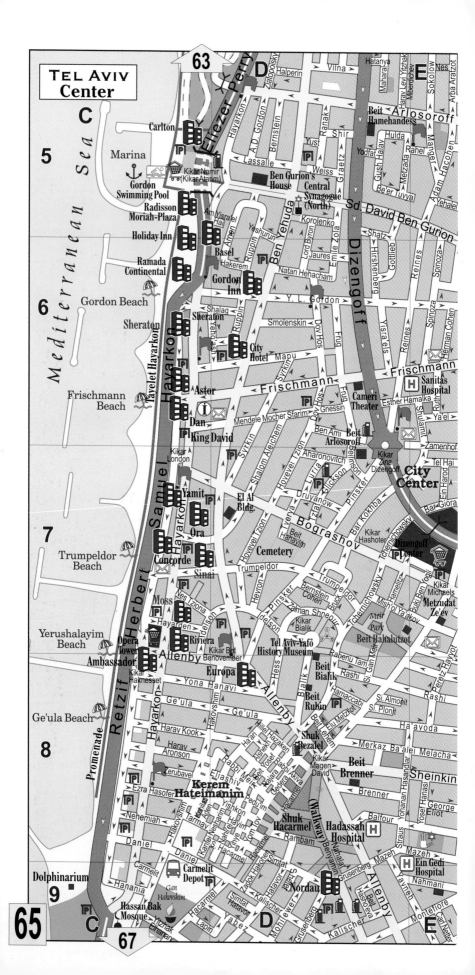

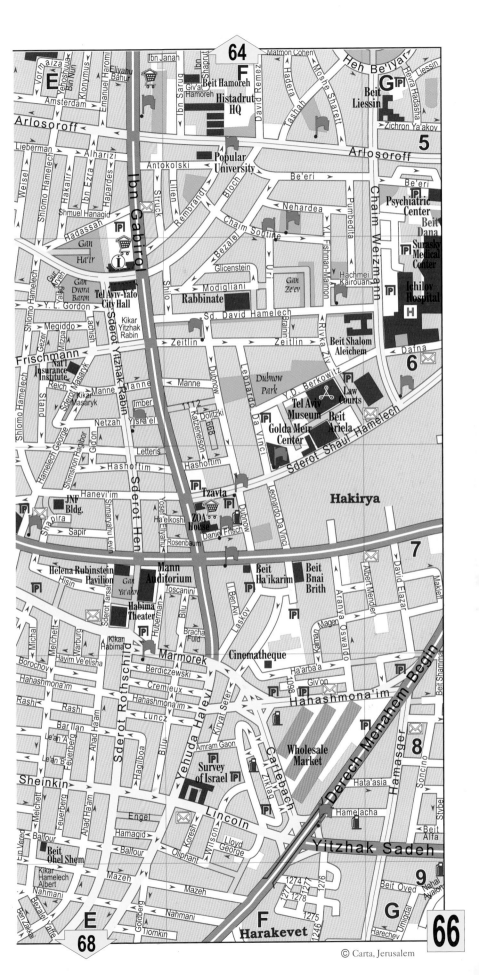

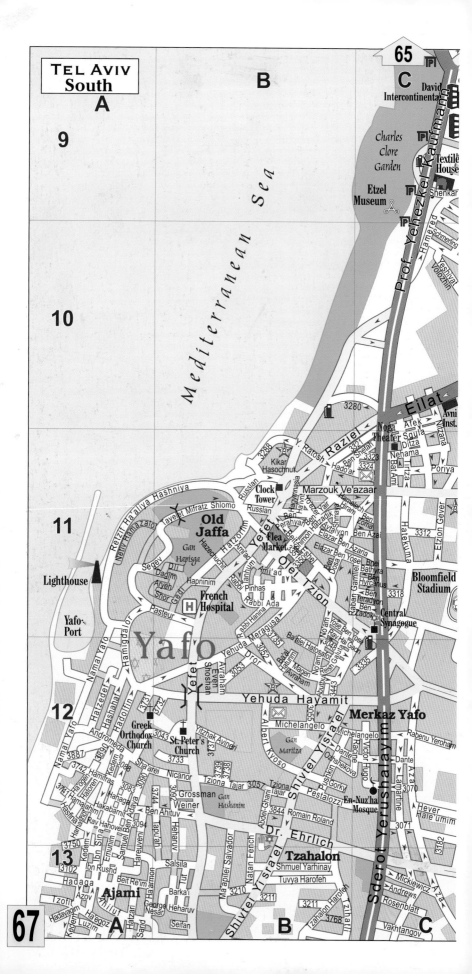

TEL AVIV
South

A   B   C

9

David
Intercontinental

Charles
Clore
Garden

Etzel
Museum

Textile
House

Shenkar

Prof. Yehezkel Kaufmann

Hanered
Schmerling

Yeshivat
Volozhin

10

Mediterranean Sea

Eilat

3280

Avni
Inst.

Nzzana

Raziel

Noga
Theater

Atek
Squia

Ben Shetah

3321

Ditza

Nehama

Poriya

3323

Bat Ami

Tirtza

3324

Hado'ar

11

Lighthouse

Yafo
Port

Reizit Ha aliya Hashniya

Netiv Hamazalot

Tayelet Mifratz Shlomo

Old
Jaffa

Gan
Hapisga

Hatzorim

Segev

Dadim

Aryeh

Shor Gedi

Hapnimim

Pasteur

Hamigdalor

Kikar
Hasochnut

Russian

3288

Russian

Clock
Tower

Russlan

Flea
Market

French
Hospital

Yefet

Ami'ad

Hahuma

Rabbi Pinhas

Rabbi Ada

Rabbi Hanina

Ole Tzion

Marzouk Ve'azaar

Perahya

Beit Eshel

Elazar Ben Yose

Shimon Hatzadik

Avtalyon

Elazar Ben Azaria

Dosa

Ben
Pornat

Bnei
Bethyra

Ben
Hyrcanus

Bloomfield
Stadium

3312

Elzion Gever

Halekuma

3318

Ben
Teradyon

Ben
Tzadok

Central
Synagogue

Yafo

Yehuda Meragusa 3735

Avraham
Event
Shoshan

Dror

3052

3053

Ba'alei Halosafot

Rav Hai Gaon

Resh Galuta

3335

3343

Yose Ben Yose

Nogah

12

Hatzedek

Hashahar

Hadolfin

3731

3732

Greek
Orthodox
Church

Andromeda

Keden

3043

3058

Sha'arei

Nicanor

St. Peter's
Church

Yitzhak Avineri

3131

3733

Namal Yafo

Hamifras

3887

3680

3090

Keden

Tziona Tajar

Yehuda Hayamit

Michelangelo

Gan
Maritza

Albert Kyoso

Merkaz Yafo

Michelangelo

Dante

Oahshekova

Victor Hugo

Gorky

Puskin

Rabenu Yeroham

Racine

Dante

Lamartine

Aza

3070

Shivtei Yisrael

Sderot Yerushalayim

13

3742

3741

Hamagdim

Hasfina

Hatzvi

Hagomen

Hakabarnit

Rav Hahovel

3083

3082

3094

Hadaga

Ben Ahituv

Heharuv

Ben Atava

Weiner

Grossman

Gan
Hashanim

Tziona Tajar

3057

Pestalozzi

Romain Roland

Dr. Ehrlich

3071

3182

En-Nuz'ha
Mosque

Aza

Hever
Hale umim

Emunim

Samuel Ben Adaya

Harelweveni

Iaqutah

Salsila

Tzahalon

Shmuel Yarhinay

Tuvya Harofeh

Mickiewicz

Andrews

Rosenblatt

3102

Hadaga

Azov

Ajami

Ahilut

Azar

Haarmon

Beit Re'im

Ibn Rushd

Kedem

Ibn Sina

Tut

Barka'i

George
Nesar

Salvador

Natan Fench

Ma'apilei

3210

3211

3211

3768

Tzahalon Harofeh

Tzihali

Vakhtangov

Tzofit

Hadavagim

Kedem

Luzim

Ha'egoz

Sajid

Seifan

Heharuv

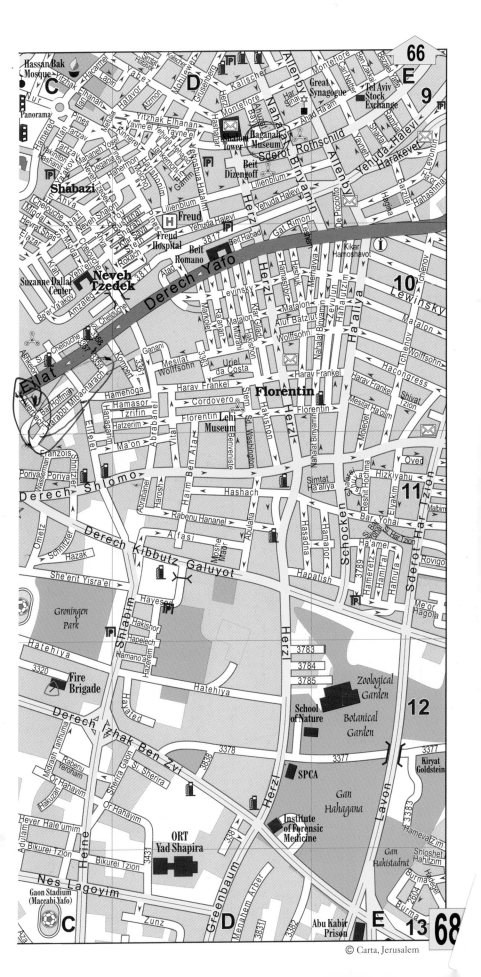

Abrabanel..........59/60 C3
Abramsky 61/62 D1
Abulafia 59/60 C2
Adani, Harav . 61/62 D1
Adhan 61/62 E2
Adler 61/62 D2
Admon 61/62 E2
Admoni 61/62 D-E3
Afodi 59/60 C3-4
Agan, Harav ... 61/62 D2
Agrippas ....
  59/60 C-D 1-2
Agron, Gershon ....
  61/62 D3
Ahad Ha'am ....
  61/62 D3-4
Alboher 61/62 D2
Alfandari 59/60 C1
Alfasi 59/60 C3-4
Algazi 59/60 C-D1
Alharizi 59/60 C-D3
Ali Ibn Abu Taleb ....
  61/62 E-F1
Alkalai 61/62 D4
Alma 59/60 C2
Alsheikh 61/62 D1
Aluf Shaltiel ....
  59/60 B-C 1-2
Alwan 59/60 C1
Amelim 61/62 E1
Anatot 59/60 C2
Antokolski 59/60 C3
Antonia 61/62 F2
Apostles 61/62 E2
Ararat 61/62 E3
Aristobulus 61/62 D2
Arlosoroff ... 61/62 D3-4
Armenian Patriarchate ...
  61/62 E3
Arnon 59/60 C2
Arvana Hayevusi ....
  61/62 E4
Asaf, Kikar 59/60 C4
Auerbach 61/62 D1
Auster, Kikar .. 61/62 D3
Avida 61/62 D3
Avigdori 61/62 D1
Avisar 59/60 C1
Avodat Yisra'el ....
  61/62 D1
Aza (Gaza), Derech ....
  59/60 C3-4
Ba'al Hatania .. 61/62 E1
Bachar, Nissim ....
  59/60 C2
Badhab 61/62 E4
Bahran 61/62 D1
Balfour 61/62 D4
Balfour (Giv'at Ram) ......
  59/60 A2-3
Bank Yisrael 59/60 B2
Bar Lev, Haim, Sderot ......
  61/62 E1
Bar Zakkai 59/60 C3
Bar'am, Kikar 61/62 D2
Barquq 61/62 F2
Baruch, Harav Shmuel ....
  59/60 B-C1
Baruchov 61/62 D2
Batei Mahasse 61/62 F3
Batei Mahasse, Kikar ......
  61/62 F3
Batei Varsha ... 61/62 D1

Be'er Sheva 59/60 C2
Be'eri 61/62 D2
Beit David 61/62 D2
Beit El 61/62 F3
Beit Habad .. 61/62 E2-3
Beit Haknesset 61/62 D2
Beit Tzur 59/60 C2
Beit Ya'akov ....
  59/60 C1-2
Beit Yisra'el 61/62 E1
Beit Yo'etz 61/62 E3
Belilios 61/62 D1
Belzer 61/62 D1
Ben Amram 61/62 D1
Ben Baruch ... 61/62 D2
Ben Hillel 61/62 D2
Ben Labrat 59/60 C4
Ben Maimon, Sderot ......
  59/60 C3
Ben Neria 59/60 C2
Ben Saruk 59/60 C4
Ben Shadad 61/62 E2
Ben Shimon ... 61/62 D3
Ben Sira 61/62 D2-3
Ben Yehuda 59/60 C-D2
Ben Zvi, Sderot ....
  59/60 C2
Berlin, Harav . 59/60 C4
Bezalel 59/60 C2
Bianchini 61/62 D2
Bibas 59/60 C2
Binyamin Mitudela ....
  59/60 C4
Birav 59/60 C2
Birnbaum 61/62 D1
Blecher 61/62 D-E1
Bloomfield . 61/62 D-E4
Bnei Brith 61/62 D2
Botta, Paul Emil ....
  61/62 D-E3
Brenner 61/62 D3-4
Brodetsky ... 59/60 A-B3
Buchachin 61/62 D2
Burj Laqlaq 61/62 F2
Burla, Yehuda 59/60 B4
Bustami 61/62 F2
Casa Nova 61/62 E3
Chelouche .. 59/60 C1-2
Cheshin 61/62 D2
Chile, Kikar 61/62 D4
Christian Quarter ....
  61/62 E3
Churches 61/62 E2
Cohen, Ephraim ....
  61/62 D1
Cohen, Ephraim, Kikar ....
  61/62 D4
Coresh 61/62 E2
Dalton 59/60 C2
Daniel Hanavi 61/62 E2
Darom 61/62 D2
David 61/62 E3
David Hamelech (King
  David) .. 61/62 D-E 3-4
Davidson, Yosef ....
  59/60 B4
Dayyan, Leib .. 61/62 D1
Degel Reuven 59/60 A1
Di Zahav, Efraim, Kikar .
  61/62 D2
Dinovitch 59/60 C1
Diskin 59/60 C3
Disraeli 61/62 D4

Dorot Rishonim ....
  61/62 D2
Du Nawas 61/62 D2
Duchan, Kikar ....
  61/62 D3
Dvir 59/60 C2
Dvora Hanevi'a ....
  61/62 E2
Edelman 61/62 D-E1
Eilat 59/60 C2
Ein Ya'akov 61/62 D-E1
El-Akhtal 61/62 F1
El-Asfahani 61/62 F2
El-Hakari 61/62 F3
Elhanan, Yitzhak ....
  61/62 D4
El-Hariri 61/62 F1
Eli'el, Dror 61/62 E3
Eliash 61/62 D2
Eliot, George .. 61/62 D3
Elisha 61/62 E2
El-Khanqa 61/62 E2
El-Mas'udi .. 61/62 F1-2
El-Mu'azamiya ....
  61/62 F2
El-Qirami 61/62 F3
El-Wad (Hagai) ....
  61/62 E-F 2-3
El-Ya'aqubi 61/62 F1
Elyashar 61/62 D2
Elyashar (Giv'at Ram) .....
  59/60 A4
Emet Leya'akov ....
  61/62 D1
Entebbi 59/60 C2-3
Es-Saraya 61/62 F3
Estori Haparhi 61/62 D1
Ethiopia 61/62 D1-2
Et-Tuta 61/62 E-F2
Etz Hayim ... 59/60 C1-2
Even Sapir 59/60 C2
Even Shoshan, Kikar ......
  61/62 D2
Even Yehoshua ....
  61/62 D1
Ezer Yoldot ... 61/62 D1
Ezrat Yisra'el .. 61/62 D2
Ez-Zahra 61/62 F1
Freres 61/62 E3
Frumkin 61/62 D2
Ga'altiyon, Kikar ....
  59/60 C4
Gal'ed 61/62 F3
Gamzu 61/62 D1
Gaon 59/60 C1
Gat, Ben Tzion ....
  59/60 A1
Gesher Hahayim ....
  59/60 C1
Geva 59/60 C2
Gezer 59/60 C2
Giv'on 59/60 C2
Granot, Avraham ....
  59/60 B4
Greek Patriarchate ....
  61/62 E3
Gruzenberg 61/62 D-E2
Ha'afarsek 59/60 C2
Ha'agas 59/60 C1
Ha'aliya 59/60 B1-2
Ha'amarkalim ....
  59/60 C-D1
Ha'ari 59/60 C4

Ha'armonim ... 59/60 C2
Ha'ayin Heth .. 61/62 E2
Ha'erez 59/60 C2
Ha'eshkol 59/60 C2
Ha'ilui 59/60 A1
Habad 61/62 E3
Habreicha 61/62 E4
Habshush 61/62 D1
Hachnasat Orhim ....
  61/62 E1
Hadaya, Ovadia ....
  59/60 C1
Hadekel 59/60 C1-2
Hafetz Hayim 61/62 D1
Hagalil 59/60 C2
Hage'onim 59/60 C3
Hagidem 59/60 C2
Hagilboa 59/60 C2
Hagitit 61/62 F3
Hagiz 61/62 D1
Hagra 59/60 C3
Hahavatzelet .. 61/62 D2
Hahermon 59/60 C2
Haherut (Davidka), Kikar
  59/60 C2
Hahistadrut ... 61/62 D2
Hahoma Hashlishit ....
  61/62 E1-2
Hakalir 59/60 C3
Hakara'im 61/62 F3
Hakarmel 59/60 C2
Hakotel 61/62 F3
Hala'or, Kikar 59/60 C3
Halev Ha'ivri . 61/62 D4
Halevanon 59/60 C2
Halhul 59/60 C2
Hama'alot ... 59/60 C-D2
Hama'aravim 61/62 D3
Hamabit 61/62 D1
Hamadrasa . 61/62 E-F3
Hamadregot ... 59/60 C2
Hamasger 61/62 D1
Hamechess, Kikar ....
  61/62 D3
Hamelacha 61/62 D1
Hametzuda 61/62 E3
Hamevaser 61/62 E4
Hamigdal 61/62 E3
Hamishlat 61/62 E3-4
Hamuse'onim, Sderot .....
  59/60 A-B 2-3
Hanagar 61/62 E1
Hanan 61/62 E2
Hanasi 59/60 C-D4
Hanatziv 59/60 C2
Hanevi'im 61/62 D-E2
Hanitzan 59/60 B1
Har Tzion 61/62 E4
Harabad 59/60 C-D3
Haran 59/60 C3
Haridbaz 61/62 D1
Harlap, Harav 59/60 C4
Harokah 61/62 D1-2
Harun er-Rashid ....
  61/62 F1-2
Haselah 59/60 C3
Hashaked 59/60 C2
Hashalshelet .. 61/62 F3
Hashezif 59/60 C2
Hashikma .. 59/60 C1-2
Hashiryon, Ma'aleh ......
  59/60 C3-4

Hashla 59/60 C3
Hasidei Karlin 61/62 D-E1
Hasoreg 61/62 D2
Hasson, Uzi 61/62 D2
Hatahana 61/62 E4
Hatam Sofer 59/60 C3
Hatamid 61/62 F3
Hatapu'ah 59/60 C1
Hatem et-Tawi 61/62 F1
Hatenu'a Hatzionit, Kikar 61/62 D3
Hatibonim 59/60 C4
Hatikva 61/62 E3
Hativat Etzioni 61/62 E4
Hativat Yerushalayim 61/62 E4
Haturim 59/60 C1
Hatut 59/60 C2
Hatzanhanim 61/62 E2
Hatzor 59/60 C2
Hatzrif Ha'adom 61/62 F2
Ha'uma, Sderot 59/60 B1
Havakuk 61/62 D1
Hayabok 59/60 C2
Hayarkon 59/60 C2
Hayarmuk 59/60 C2
Hayehudim 61/62 F3
Hayei Adam 61/62 D1
Hayim 59/60 C2
Hazanovitch 61/62 D1
Hazaz, Hayim, Sderot 59/60 C3-4
Heharash 61/62 D1
Heil Hahandasa 61/62 F1-2
Heleni Hamalka 61/62 D-E2
Herzl, Sderot 59/60 A 1-3
Herzog, Harav 59/60 A-C 4-16
Hesed Le'avraham 61/62 D1
Hess 61/62 D3
Hevrat Shas 61/62 D-E1
Hevrat Tehilim 61/62 D1
Hillel 61/62 D2
Hirschenberg 59/60 C2-3
Honi Hame'agel 61/62 D1
Hovevei Tzion 61/62 D4
Hulda Hanevi'a 61/62 E2
Hyrcanus 61/62 D2
Ibn Batuta 61/62 F1
Ibn Ezra 59/60 C3
Ibn Gabirol 61/62 D3
Ibn Khaldun 61/62 F1
Ibn Shaprut 59/60 C3
Ibn Sina 59/60 C3
ICA, Kikar 59/60 B3
Iddo Hanavi 61/62 E2
Ikhwan es-Safa 61/62 F1
Ilan 59/60 C1
Iraqi 59/60 C2
Iron Gate 61/62 F2
Israels 59/60 C3
Jabotinsky, Ze'ev 61/62 D4
Kafah 61/62 D1
Kahanov 59/60 C3

Kaplan, Eliezer 59/60 B2-3
Karib, Yitzhak 61/62 E3
Katz 61/62 E1
Keren Hayesod 61/62 D3
Keren Kayemet Leyisra'el (K.K.L.) 59/60 C-D3
Kfar Bar'am 59/60 C2
Kfar Nahum 59/60 C1
Khaldiya 61/62 F3
Khalid Ibn el-Walid 61/62 F1
Khulda 61/62 E3
Ki'ah 59/60 C2
Kinneret 59/60 C1
Kiryat Moshe 59/60 A1
Kiss, Naomi 61/62 E1-2
Kook, Harav 61/62 D2
Korazin 59/60 C2
Korot Ha'itim 59/60 A1
Lachish 59/60 C2
Lampronti 59/60 B1
Latin Patriarchate 61/62 E3
Lazar, Moshe Ve'esther 61/62 E1
Levi Itzhak Miberdichev 61/62 D1
Levi, Meir, Kikar 59/60 C2
Levush Mordecai 61/62 D1
Lilian Promenade 59/60 B3-4
Lincoln 61/62 D3
Lindner 61/62 D1
Lod 59/60 C2
Lorch, Netanel 59/60 A-B2
Lotan, Kikar 59/60 B1
Luncz 61/62 D2
Ma'aleh Hashalom 61/62 F3-4
Ma'alot Ir David 61/62 F3-4
Maccabi Mutzerai, Kikar 61/62 D2
Magnes, Kikar 59/60 C4
Magnes, Sderot 59/60 A3-4
Mahaneh Yehuda 59/60 C1-2
Mahoza 61/62 E1
Maimon, Harav 59/60 A-B1
Maiser Promenade 59/60 B3
Malchizedek 61/62 F3-4
Malkhi 61/62 E3-4
Mani, Eliyahu 59/60 C1
Maon 59/60 C2
Mapu 61/62 D3-4
Marcus, David 61/62 D4
Mattityahu, Kikar 59/60 C2
Mawlawiya 61/62 F2
Mazie 59/60 C-D2
Mazkeret Moshe 59/60 C2
Mazor 59/60 C1
Me'a She'arim 61/62 D1
Meir, Ya'akov 61/62 D1
Meiron 59/60 C1
Menahem 59/60 C1
Menashe Ben Yisra'el 61/62 D2-3

Mendele Mocher Sfarim 61/62 D4
Menora 59/60 C2
Mesilat Yesharim 59/60 C-D2
Meyuhas 59/60 C1
Misgav Ladach 61/62 F3
Mishkenot 59/60 C2
Mishmerot 61/62 E2
Mitzpeh 59/60 C2
Modi'in 59/60 C1
Mohilewer, Kikar 59/60 C3
Molcho 61/62 D4
Molcho, Kikar 59/60 C3
Monbaz 61/62 D2
Muristan 61/62 E3
Mussaief, Shlomo 61/62 D1
Na'amat, Kikar 61/62 D1
Nachon 61/62 E3-4
Nafha 61/62 D1
Nahalat Shiv'a 61/62 D2
Nahalat Tzadok 59/60 C3
Nahman Mibreslav 61/62 D1
Narkiss 59/60 C2
Nasi, Don Yosef 59/60 C1
Natan Hanavi 61/62 E2
Navon 59/60 C1
Nayot 59/60 B4
Netiv Yitzhak 59/60 C1
Neveh Sha'anan 59/60 B4
New Gate 61/62 E2-3
Nezivim 61/62 E1
Nibarta 59/60 B1
Nordau 59/60 B1
Nordau, Kikar 59/60 B1
Nov 59/60 C2
Nur ed-Din 61/62 F2
Ohel Moshe 59/60 C2
Ohel Shlomo 59/60 C1
Omar Ibn el-As 61/62 E1
Omari 61/62 F2
Oneg Shabat 61/62 E1
Orde, Kikar 61/62 D4
Orenstein 59/60 C1
Otzar Hasfarim 61/62 E1
Ovadia Mibertinoro 61/62 D3-4
Pe'at Hashulhan 61/62 D1
Peki'in 59/60 C1
Peleh Yo'etz 61/62 E3
Pelet 61/62 E3
Peres 61/62 D1
Pick 59/60 A1-2
Pierotti 61/62 E2
Pikud Hamerkaz 61/62 E1
Pikud Hamerkaz, Kikar 61/62 E1
Pines 61/62 D1
Plugat Hakotel 61/62 F3
Plumer, Kikar 61/62 D4
Poliakov 59/60 A1-2
Porush 59/60 C3
Prague 61/62 D2
Pri Hadash 61/62 D1
Rabbi Akiva 61/62 D2-3
Rabbi Aryeh 59/60 C2

Rabbi Shlomo 61/62 D-E1
Rabenu Tam 59/60 C-D1
Radak 59/60 C3-4
Rafa'el Hakohen, Kikar 61/62 D2
Ralbah 61/62 D1
Rama 59/60 C2
Ramban 59/60 C3
Raphael, Ezra 59/60 C2
Rasas 61/62 E2
Rashba 59/60 C3
Rashbam 59/60 C1
Rashi 59/60 C1
Ratzabi 61/62 D1
Refaeli 59/60 C2
Reines, Harav 59/60 A1
Reishit Hochma 61/62 D1
Rivlin 61/62 D2-3
Rivlin, Kikar 59/60 C3
Rosenthal 61/62 D1
Rothenberg 59/60 C4
Rothschild 59/60 B3
Rubin, Reuven, Kikar 61/62 E3
Ruppin, Derech 59/60 B-C3
Sa'adiya 61/62 F2
Saadiah Gaon 59/60 C3-4
Sachs 61/62 E1
Safra, Kikar 61/62 D2
Salah ed-Din 61/62 E-F1
Salahiya 61/62 F2
Salant, Harav Shmuel 61/62 D-E 1-2
Salman, E. 61/62 D2
Salomon 61/62 D2
Samuel, Herbert 61/62 D2
Schatz 59/60 C-D2
Schick, Conrad 61/62 E2
Schwartz 59/60 C1
Sdei Hemed 59/60 C-D1
Sfat Emet 59/60 C1
Sha'ar Ha'arayot, Derech 61/62 F2
Sha'ar Haprahim 61/62 F2
Sha'ar Shechem, Kikar 61/62 E2
Sha'arei Hesed 59/60 C3
Sha'arei Mishpat 59/60 B2
Sha'arei Moshe 61/62 D1
Sha'arei Tzedek 59/60 C1
Shabazi 59/60 C2
Shacham 61/62 D2
Shadal 59/60 C1
Shaddad 61/62 D2
Shalom Aleichem 61/62 D4
Shamai 61/62 D2
Sharabi 61/62 D1
Shazar, Sderot 59/60 B1
Shechem, Derech 61/62 E-F 1-2
Sheikh Hasan 61/62 F2
Sheikh Rihan 61/62 F2
Shema 61/62 E3
Shevet Tzedek 59/60 C1
Shfar'am 59/60 C2
Shiloh 59/60 C2

Shim'on Ben Shetah ... 61/62 D2
Shirizli ... 59/60 C2
Shivtei Yisra'el ... 61/62 E2
Shlomo Hamelech ... 61/62 D-E 2-3
Shlomtzion Hamalka ... 61/62 D2-3
Shmuel Hanagid ... 59/60 C2-3
Shoham ... 61/62 D2
Sholal ... 61/62 D1
Shomrei Emunim ... 61/62 E1
Shomron ... 59/60 C2
Shoshan ... 61/62 E2
Simon, Derech ... 59/60 A4
Smolenskin ... 61/62 D3
Sokolow ... 61/62 D3-4
Soloveichik ... 61/62 D1
Somekh, Ovadia ... 59/60 C2
Spitzer ... 61/62 E1
St. Demetrius ... 61/62 E3
St. Francis ... 61/62 E3
St. George ... 61/62 E1

St. George (Old City) ... 61/62 E3
St. Mark ... 61/62 E3
St. Peter ... 61/62 E3
Steinhardt, Hatzayar ... 61/62 E3
Stoynovsky ... 61/62 D2
Straus, Kikar ... 61/62 E2
Straus, Nathan ... 61/62 D1-2
Sultan Suleiman ... 61/62 F2
Suq ed-Dabbagha ... 61/62 E3
Syrkin ... 59/60 A1
Tahkemoni ... 59/60 C1
Tarmav ... 61/62 D1
Tashbetz ... 59/60 C1
Tavor ... 59/60 C2
Tekoa ... 59/60 C2
Tel Or, Kikar ... 59/60 C3
Ticho, Mevo ... 61/62 D2
Tiferet Yisra'el 61/62 F3
Touro ... 61/62 E3
Tverya ... 59/60 C2
Tzahal, Kikar ... 61/62 E2-3
Tzarfat, Kikar 61/62 D3

Tzfat ... 59/60 C2
Tzion, Kikar ... 61/62 D2
Tzipori ... 59/60 C2
Tzo'ar ... 59/60 C2
Usha ... 59/60 C2
Ussishkin ... 59/60 C3
Valero ... 59/60 C1
Via Dolorosa ... 61/62 E-F2
Vilnay, Ze'ev ... 59/60 A2
Wadi Hilwa 61/62 F3-4
Wallach, Moshe ... 59/60 B1
Wallenberg ... 61/62 D2
Washington ... 61/62 D3
Wise ... 59/60 B3
Wolffsohn, David, Sderot ... 59/60 A2
Yabez ... 61/62 D2
Yafo ... 59/60 B-E 1-2
Yalon, Hanoch ... 59/60 C2-3
Yana'it, Rahel, Kikar ... 59/60 C3
Yanai ... 61/62 D-E3
Yehuda Hamaccabi ... 59/60 C1
Yehudit ... 59/60 C1

Yellin, David ... 59/60 C-D1
Yemin Moshe . 61/62 E4
Yesha'yahu ... 61/62 D1
Yeshu'at Ya'akov ... 61/62 D-E1
Yifhan ... 61/62 D1
Yitzhak Rabin, Sderot ... 59/60 B1-2
Yitzhari ... 61/62 D1
Yohanan Hasandlar ... 61/62 D1
Yohanan Migush Halav .. 61/62 E2
Yosef ... 59/60 C2
Yosef Ben Mattityahu ... 59/60 C1
Zamenhof ... 61/62 D3
Zecharia Harofeh ... 61/62 D1
Zichron Tuvia 59/60 C2
Zmora ... 61/62 D2
Zussman, Yoel 59/60 B2

Index of Streets of TEL AVIV (pages 63-68)

Abdel-Ghani 67/68 B12
Abrabanel ... 67/68 D10-11
Abulafia ... 67/68 D11
Abutbul ... 67/68 B12
Adam Hacohen65/66 E5
Adulam ...67/68 C12-13
Afek ... 67/68 C10
Afyter ... 63/64 F1
Agnon ...63/64 E-F2
Agrippas ... 63/64 E3
Ahad Ha'am 65/66 E8
Aharonovitch. 65/66 D7
Ahavat Tzion .. 63/64 G4
Ahiluf ... 67/68 A13
Ahuzat Bayit .. 67/68 D9
Ahva ... 67/68 C10
Akiva , Aryeh 63/64 G4
Alexander Yannai ... 63/64 E3-4
Alfasi ... 67/68 D11
Alharizi ... 65/66 E5
Alkalai ... 63/64 E4
Allenby .. 65/66 D-E 7-9
Almonit, Simta65/66 D8
Alroy ...67/68 C-D9
Alshekh ... 65/66 D8
Aluf Batzlut ... 67/68 D10-11
Am Yisra'el Hai ... 65/66 C-D5
Ami'el, Harav ... 63/64 F-G3
Ami'ad ... 67/68 B11
Amos ... 63/64 E4
Amos, Simta 63/64 E4
Amram Gaon, Rav ... 65/66 F8
Amsterdam ... 65/66 E5
Amzaleg ... 67/68 C10
Andrews ... 67/68 C13
Andromeda .. 67/68 A12
Antigonus ... 63/64 F4

Antokolski ...65/66 E-F5
Arba Aratzot ... 65/66 E5
Arber, Menahem ... 67/68 D13
Aristobulus ... 63/64 F3
Arlosoroff ... 65/66 E-G5
Arnon ... 65/66 D5-6
Aronson, Harav ... 65/66 C8
Ashkelon ... 67/68 C10
Atad ... 67/68 D10
Atarim, Kikar - see Namir, Kikar
Atzmon ... 67/68 D9
Auerbach ... 67/68 C10
Avineri, Yitzhak ... 67/68 B12
Avtalyon ... 67/68 B11
Aza ... 67/68 C12-13
Azarya ... 63/64 E5
Azov ... 67/68 A13
Ba'al Haturim67/68 B12
Ba'alei Hatosafot ... 67/68 B11-12
Bahur, Eliyahu 65/66 E5
Balfour ... 65/66 D-E8
Bar Giora ... 65/66 E7
Bar Hoffman 67/68 C10
Bar Ilan, Harav65/66 E8
Bar Kokhba ... 65/66 D7
Bar Yohai ...67/68 E11
Bar Yohai, Simta ... 67/68 E11
Bareli ... 63/64 F1
Barka'i ... 67/68 B13
Barnett ... 67/68 C10
Barzilai ... 67/68 E9
Basel ... 63/64 D-E4
Bat Ami ... 67/68 C11
Be'er Tuvya 65/66 D-E5
Be'er Ya'akov67/68 C10
Be'eri ...65/66 F-G5
Begin, Menahem,

Derech .. 65/66 E-F 8-9
Beilinson ... 65/66 D7
Beit Alfa ... 65/66 G8
Beit Eshel ... 67/68 B11
Beit Habad ...67/68 D10
Beit Hahayim. 65/66 D7
Beit Hasho'eva67/68 D9
Beit Lehem ... 65/66 D8
Beit Oved ... 65/66 G9
Beit Re'im ... 67/68 A13
Beit Shammai. 65/66 G8
Beit Yosef ... 65/66 D8
Belkind ... 63/64 F4
Ben Ahituv67/68 A-B12
Ben Ami ... 65/66 D6
Ben Asher ...67/68 E11
Ben Atar, Haim ... 67/68 D11
Ben Avi, I. ... 65/66 F7
Ben Azai ... 67/68 C11
Ben Dosa ... 67/68 B11
Ben Gurion, David, Sderot ... 65/66 D-E 5-6
Ben Hillel ... 63/64 G1
Ben Hyrcanus ... 67/68 C11
Ben Perahiyah ... 67/68 B11
Ben Shetah67/68 B-C11
Ben Sira ... 63/64 G3
Ben Teradyon67/68 C11
Ben Tzion, Sderot ... 65/66 E7
Ben Yair ... 67/68 B11
Ben Yehuda 63/64 D4-7
Ben Zadok ... 67/68 E9
Ben Zakkai ... 67/68 E9
Ben Zoma ... 67/68 C11
Ben Zvi, Izhak, Derech... 67/68 C-F 12-13
Benveniste ... 67/68 D10-11
Berdiczewski65/66 E-F8

Berkowitz, Y. D. ... 65/66 F6
Bernstein ... 65/66 D5
Bernstein-Cohen ... 65/66 D7
Bet Benovember, Kikar ... 65/66 C-D 7-8
Bezalel ... 65/66 F5-6
Bialik ... 65/66 D8
Bialik, Kikar ... 65/66 D7
Bikurei Tzion67/68 C-D 12-13
Biltmore ... 63/64 F4
Bilu ... 65/66 E-F 7-8
Birnbaum ... 63/64 G3
Bloch ... 65/66 F5-6
Bnei Bathyra 67/68 C11
Bnei Dan ...63/64 F-G3
Bnei Moshe 63/64 G3
Bodenheimer, Dr. ... 63/64 F3-4
Bograshov ... 65/66 D7
Bonei Ha'ir ... 63/64 E2
Borochov ...65/66 E8
Brainin ... 65/66 F6
Brandeis ... 63/64 F3-4
Brenner ... 65/66 D8
Bruck ... 65/66 D7
Bublick ... 63/64 F3
Buki Ben Yogli 65/66 E7
Burma ...67/68 E13
Bustanai ...67/68 D9-10
Byron, Lord 65/66 D5-6
Carlebach ... 65/66 F8
Carmelit ... 67/68 C9
Chelouche, Simta ... 67/68 C-D 9-10
Cohen, Herman ... 65/66 E6
Cordova ... 63/64 E5
Cordovero ...67/68 D10
Costa, Uriel da ... 67/68 D10

Cremieux......65/66E-F8
Da Costa, Uriel......
67/68D10
Da Vinci, Leonardo......
65/66F6-7
Dafna......65/66G6
Dagim......67/68A11-12
Daniel......65/66CC-D8
Danin......63/64G4
Dante......67/68B12
David Hamelech, Sderot
65/66F6
De Haas......63/64F4
De Picciotto......
67/68E9-10
Degania......67/68C-D9
Ditza......67/68C11
Dizengoff......63/64D-E
4-7
Dizengoff, Zina, Kikar....
65/66D7
Dli......67/68B11
Dolitzki......65/66F6
Dror......67/68B12
Druyanow......65/66D7
Dubnow......65/66F6-7
Ehrlich, Dr...67/68B12
Eilat......67/68C10
Ein Dor......65/66G7
Ein Ganim......67/68D9
Ein Gedi......63/64E4
Ein Harod......65/66E7
Ein Vered......65/66E8
Ein Ya'akov......67/68C9
Elazar Ben Azaria......
67/68B-C11
Elazar Ben Yose......
67/68B-C11
Elazar Hahorani......
63/64F3
Elazar......67/68C9-10
Elazar, David.65/66G7
Elhanan, Yitzhak......
67/68C-D9
Eliashiv......65/66D8
Elifelet......65/68C10-11
Eliot, George...65/66E8
Elu Metzi'ot...65/66D8
Elyakim......67/68E11
Emanuel Haromi......
65/66E5
Emden......63/64E4
Emunim..67/68A12-13
Engel......65/66E8
Epstein......63/64F4
Esther Hamalka......
65/66D-E6
Estori Haparhi 63/64E4
Etzion Gever 67/68C11
Even Shoshan, Avraham
67/68B12
Eybeschuetz....63/64E4
Ezra Hasofer..65/66C8
Feivel......63/64G5
Fench, Natan 67/68B13
Feuerberg......65/66E8
Fishman-Maimon, Y.L....
65/66F5-6
Florentin...67/68D-E10
Francoise......67/68C11
Frankel, Harav......
67/68D-E10
Frankfurt...63/64D4-5
Franzois......67/68C11
Friedman, Harav......
63/64G3
Frisch, Daniel..65/66F7

Frischmann 65/66D-E6
Frug......65/66D6
Fuld, Bracha....65/66F7
Galili......63/64E-F2
Gan Meir, Simta......
65/66D7-8
Ganani......67/68D10
Gat Rimon 67/68D9-10
Ge'ula......65/66C-D8
Gedera......65/66D8
Gedi......67/68B11
Gerizim......63/64D4
Gezer......65/66E6
Gid'on......65/66E6-7
Giv'at Hamoreh......
65/66F5
Giv'on......65/66F8
Glicenstein......65/66F6
Glickson......65/66D7
Gluskin......63/64G4
Gnessin......65/66D6
Goldberg......65/66E9
Goldman......67/68B10
Gordon, A. D. 65/66D5
Gordon, Y. L.......
65/66D-E6
Gorky......67/68B12
Gottlieb......65/66D6
Graetz......65/66D5
Greenbaum..67/68D13
Gronemann....63/64G1
Grossman......67/68B12
Grusenberg....67/68D9
Gur Aryeh......65/66E6
Gur, Yehuda..63/64G4
Gush Halav...65/66D5
Gvulot......67/68D10
Ha'aliya......67/68E10
Ha'aliya, Simta......
67/68D-E11
Ha'arba'a......65/66F8
Ha'ari......65/66D8
Ha'armon.67/68A-B13
Ha'avoda....65/66D-E8
Ha'egoz......67/68A13
Ha'elkoshi....65/66E-F7
Ha'ogen......67/68A12
Ha'or......67/68E9
Habashan......63/64E4
Habima, Kikar 65/66E7
Hacarmel......65/66C-D
8-9
Hacarmel, Simta......
65/66D8
Hachmei Kairouan......
65/66F-G6
Hadaga......67/68A13
Hadassah......65/66E5-6
Hadayagim...67/68A13
Hadegel......67/68E13
Hadera......65/66F5
Hado'ar......67/68B11
Hadolfin......67/68A12
Haggai......63/64E4
Hagil'ad......63/64E4
Hagilboa......65/66E8
Hagina......67/68E9
Hagymnasia Ha'ivrit......
67/68B11
Hahaga......67/68A12
Hahalutzim...67/68E10
Hahashmal......67/68E9
Hahashmona'im......
65/66E-G8
Hahermesh...67/68E13

Hahermon..67/68C-D9
Hahovevim....63/64D5
Hai Gaon, Rav......
67/68B-C 11-12
Hakabarnit...67/68A12
Hakalir......65/66E5
Hakerem......65/66D6
Hakishon67/68D10-11
Hakishor......67/68D11
Haknesset, Kikar......
65/66C8
Hakovshim.65/66C-D8
Hakuzari......67/68C12
Halperin......65/66D5
Hama'apilim..65/66G9
Hamaccabi.....65/66D8
Hamagid......65/66E8
Hamalahim..67/68A12
Hamano'a....67/68D12
Hamanor......67/68E11
Hamasger......65/66F-G
8-9
Hamashbir...67/68D10
Hamashot....67/68A12
Hatoren......67/68A12
Hamasor......67/68D10
Hamedina, Kikar......
63/64F-G4
Hamehoga67/68C-D10
Hamelacha..65/66F-G8
Hamelech Albert, Kikar..
67/68E9
Hamelech George......
65/66D-E 6-8
Hamelech Hiram......
67/68B-C11
Hamelitz......65/66D7
Hamered...67/68C9-10
Hameretz......67/68E11
Hamevatz'im 67/68E12
Hamif'al......67/68E11
Hamifras......67/68A12
Hamigdalor......
67/68A11-12
Hamiktzo'a..65/66F-G9
Hamoshavot, Kikar......
67/68E10-11
Hanagarim......
67/68C10-11
Hanania......67/68C9
Hanevi'im......65/66E7
Hankin......63/64F4
Hapardes......65/66E5
Hapatish...67/68D-E11
Hapelech67/68D11-12
Hapninim...67/68B11
Har Nevo......63/64E4
Har Sinai......67/68D9
Har Tzion, Sderot......
67/68E11
Har Tzion, Simta......
67/68E11
Harabbi Mibacharach....
67/68C10
Harakevet.....65/66E-F9
Harari......63/64G1
Harechev......65/66G9
Hareuveni......
67/68A12-13
Harishonim...67/68D9
Harosh......67/68D11
Hartglas......63/64G1
Harutz......65/66G9
Hasadna......67/68D11
Hasfina......67/68A12
Hashach......67/68D11
Hashahaf......67/68A12

Hashahar......67/68D9
Hashanit......67/68C9
Hashla......63/64E4
Hashlosha......65/66G9
Hashoftim....65/66E-F7
Hashomron...67/68E10
Hashoter, Kikar......
65/66D7
Hashuk......67/68D10
Hasochnut, Kikar......
67/68B11
Hata'arucha...63/64D3
Hata'asia......65/66F-G8
Hatalmi......67/68D9
Hatam Sofer65/66D-E5
Hatanya......65/66D5
Hatarsi, Simta.63/64E3
Hatavor......67/68D9
Hatavor, Simta67/68D9
Hatehiya......
67/68C-D11-12
Hatekuma.....67/68C11
Hatnufa......67/68E11
Hatoren......67/68A12
Hatzari......67/68A13
Hatzedef......67/68A12
Hatzerim......67/68D10
Hatzionut......63/64G4
Hatzorfim......67/68B11
Havakuk Hanavi......
63/64D4
Hayarden......65/66C7
Hayarkon......65/66C-D
5-8
Hayarkon, Tayelet
(Promenade) 65/66C6
Hayated......67/68D12
Hayesod......67/68D11
Hayim Ve'elisha......
65/66E8
Hayim......65/66D8
Hayotman......63/64G4
Hayyot, Peretz......
65/66E7-8
Hazak......67/68C11
Hazanowitz...67/68E10
Hazechuchit.67/68B11
Hazerem......67/68D12
Hazohar......63/64G3
He'amal......67/68E11
Heftman......65/66F7
Heh Be'iyar......
63/64F-G 4-5
Heharuv.67/68B12-13
Heine......67/68C12-13
Helsinki......65/66G5
Hen, Sderot.65/66E6-7
Herzl......67/68D9-12
Herzog, Harav63/64G4
Hess......65/66D7-8
Hever Hale'umim......
67/68C12
Hevra Hadasha......
65/66G5
Hevrat Shas......
67/68C9-10
Hevron......65/66D7
Hildesheimer.63/64G3
Hill, Kikar......63/64E3
Hillel Hazaken65/66D8
Hirshenberg...65/66D6
Hisin......65/66E7
Homa Umigdal......
65/66G9
Honi Hame'agel......
63/64E-F4

Hos, Dov............ 65/66 D6
Hosea 63/64 D3
Hovevei Tzion................
65/66 D6-7
Huberman......... 65/66 E7
Hugo, Victor 67/68 C12
Hulda............. 65/66 D5
Hurshat Nuz'ha..........
67/68 C13
Ibn Ezra.......... 65/66 E5
Ibn Gabirol.....63/64 E-F
2-7
Ibn Janah......65/66 E-F5
Ibn Rushd.... 67/68 A13
Ibn Saruq......... 65/66 F5
Ibn Shaprut..... 65/66 F5
Ibn Sina..67/68 A12-13
Idelson.......65/66 C-D7
Ilan................. 67/68 C9
Imber............. 65/66 E6
Jabotinsky, Ze'ev..........
65/66 E-G 4-5
Jaures............. 65/66 D6
Kahnshtam...... 63/64 F4
Kalischer....... 67/68 D9
Kanfei Nesharim..........
65/66 C-D8
Kaph Gimel Yordei
Hasira............63/64 D3
Kaplan, Eliezer..............
65/66 F-G7
Karni, Yehuda 63/64 G1
Katzenelson. 65/66 F6-7
Kaufmann, Prof.
Yehezkel . 67/68 C9-10
Kedem.....67/68 A12-13
Kehilat Aden...............
65/66 C-D8
Keren Hayesod, Sderot....
63/64 G1
Kfar Giladi....67/68 D10
Kfar Sava......67/68 D10
Ki'ah........... 67/68 C10
Kibbutz Galuyot, Derech
67/68 C-E11
Kinneret......... 67/68 D9
Kiryat Sefer 65/66 F8
Klee 63/64 G5
Klonymus........ 65/66 E5
Kompert......67/68 D10
Kook, Harav ... 65/66 C8
Koresh............ 65/66 F8
Korolenko....... 65/66 D5
Kovner, Abba.. 63/64 E2
Kyoso, Albert 67/68 B12
Lachish 65/66 E6
Lachower 63/64 G1
Lamartine 67/68 C12
Lapin...........67/68 C-D9
Laskov........... 65/66 F7
Lassalle 65/66 D5
Lavon...........67/68 E12
Le'an 'A'........ 65/66 E8
Le'an 'B'........ 65/66 E8
Leshem.......67/68 D10
Letteris............ 65/66 E7
Levi Yitzhak
Miberdichev..................
63/64 D-E5
Levin, Shmaryahu..........
65/66 E7
Levinsky 67/68 D10
Levontin 67/68 E9
Lewinsky ..67/68 D-E10
Lieberman 65/66 E5
Liessin............ 63/64 G5

Lilien............... 65/66 F5
Lilienblum...... 67/68 D9
Lincoln............ 65/66 F8
Lipsky 63/64 F4
Lloyd George... 65/66 F8
London, Kikar 65/66 C7
Luncz...........65/66 E-F8
Luria 65/66 D7
Luzim............ 67/68 A13
Ma'apilei Salvador ....
67/68 B12-13
Ma'on 67/68 D11
Ma'or, Moshe ....
67/68 D11
Magen Avraham ....
67/68 B12
Magen David, Kikar ......
65/66 D8
Magen, Kalman ....
65/66 F7
Mahaneh Yosef ....
67/68 C-D9
Maharal........... 65/66 D5
Makleff 65/66 G7
Malachi 63/64 D4
Malbim...........67/68 E11
Mandelstam ... 63/64 D4
Manger........... 65/66 E5
Manne 65/66 E-F6
Mapu 65/66 D6
Markolet.......67/68 D10
Marmorek......65/66 E-F
7-8
Marshall 63/64 F3-4
Marzouk Ve'azaar ....
67/68 B-C11
Masaryk, Kikar65/66 E6
Masaryk, Sderot ....
65/66 E6
Matmon Cohen ....
65/66 F5
Mattityahu 63/64 F3
Mazeh.... 65/66 D-F 8-9
Me'or Hagola 67/68 E11
Megiddo 65/66 E6
Melchett 65/66 E7-8
Mendele Mocher Sfarim
65/66 E6
Mendelssohn .. 65/66 E6
Mendler, Albert ....
65/66 G7
Merhavya. 67/68 D-E10
Merkaz Ba'alei Melacha.
65/66 D-E8
Mesilat Ha'olim ....
67/68 E10
Mesilat Wolffsohn ....
67/68 D10
Metulla 67/68 C-D9
Metzada.......... 65/66 D5
Micah 63/64 D4
Micha, Simta.. 63/64 D4
Michaels, Kikar ....
65/66 E7
Michal 65/66 E7
Michelangelo...................
67/68 B-C12
Mickiewicz .. 67/68 C13
Midrash Tanhuma ....
67/68 C12
Migdal 67/68 C9-10
Mikonis.....65/66 F-G9
Milano, Rahava ....
63/64 F3
Miriam Hahashmona'it..
63/64 E3-4
Mish'ol Ya'akov.............

65/66 D-E7
Mitzpa 65/66 E6
Mizrahi.......67/68 D10
Modi'in.... 63/64 E3-4
Modigliani 65/66 F6
Mohilewer, Harav..........
67/68 D9
Molcho.......... 67/68 D9
Moledet .. 67/68 E10-11
Montefiore . 67/68 D-E9
Moser, Ya'akov63/64 F4
Mossinsohn..... 63/64 E4
Motzkin 63/64 D4
Nahalat Binyamin ....
65/66 D8-9
Nahli'el 65/66 D8
Nahmani 65/66 E-F9
Nahshon 63/64 D4
Nahum Hanavi ....
63/64 D4
Najara 65/66 D8
Namal Tel Aviv ....
63/64 D3-4
Namal Yafo .. 67/68 A12
Namir, Kikar..................
65/66 C-D5
Namir, Mordechai,
Derech ..63/64 F-G 1-5
Natan Hehacham ....
65/66 D6
Nehama 67/68 C11
Nehardea........ 65/66 F5
Nehemiah....... 65/66 C8
Nes Lagoyim ....
65/66 C-D13
Nes Tziona 65/66 C7
Nes 65/66 E5
Nesar, George ....
67/68 A-B13
Netiv Hamazalot............
67/68 A11-12
Netter, Carl 67/68 E9
Netzah Yisra'el65/66 E6
Neveh Shalom.................
67/68 C-D 9-10
Neveh Tzedek 67/68 C9
Nirim 65/66 G9
Nissenbaum 63/64 F-G3
Nitzana ...67/68 C10-11
No'am 67/68 B11-12
Nordau, Sderot63/64 E4
Nordau, Simta 63/64 E4
Nur................ 67/68 C9
Olei Tzion ... 67/68 B11
Oliphant 65/66 F8
Ometz 67/68 C11
Onkelos 63/64 G3
Or Hahayim ....
67/68 C-D12
Oswaldo, Aranya ....
65/66 F7-8
Ovadia Mibertinoro.......
63/64 E4
Ovadia............. 63/64 E4
Oved 67/68 E11
Ozhshekova....................
67/68 B-C12
Pasteur....67/68 A11-12
Pedu'im 65/66 D8
Peki'in 63/64 D4
Perry, Eliezer....................
65/66 C-D5
Pestalozzi 67/68 B12
Philo............. 65/66 E6
Pineles 63/64 F3
Pines.... 67/68 C-D 9-10
Pinkas 63/64 F-G4

Pinsker............ 65/66 D7
Plonit, Simta... 65/66 D8
Plumer, Kikar 63/64 D3
Poriya............67/68 C11
Prague 63/64 D5
Pumbedita ... 65/66 F5-6
Pushkin........ 67/68 B12
Ra'anan........67/68 D10
Raban Gamliel ....
67/68 B-C11
Rabbi Ada 67/68 B11
Rabbi Akiva.... 65/66 D8
Rabbi Hanina67/68 B11
Rabbi Meir 65/66 D8
Rabbi Pinhas 67/68 B11
Rabenu Hananel ....
67/68 D11
Rabenu Tam65/66 D7-8
Rabenu Yeroham...........
67/68 C12
Rabin, Yitzhak, Kikar......
65/66 E6
Rabin, Yitzhak, Sderot ....
65/66 E6
Racine........... 67/68 C12
Rahel 65/66 D-E5
Rambam 65/66 D8
Ramhal 67/68 E9
Ranak............. 65/66 D5
Rashi 65/66 D-E8
Ratosh, Yonatan ....
67/68 B11
Rav Hahovel. 67/68 A12
Rav Tza'ir 63/64 G3
Raziel.67/68 B-C 10-11
Reich 65/66 E6
Reines, Harav ....
65/66 D-E6
Reish Galuta. 67/68 B12
Rembrandt 65/66 F5
Remez, David...................
63/64 F4-5
Reshit Hochma ....
67/68 E11
Retzif Ha'aliya Hashniya
67/68 A11-12
Retzif Herbert Samuel.....
65/66 C6-8
Rilf................ 63/64 G3
Rishonim 67/68 D9
Rofeh Hamahtarot...........
63/64 E2
Rokach.......... 67/68 D10
Rokach, Yisra'el, Sderot...
63/64 E-G 1-2
Roland, Romain ....
67/68 B12
Rosenbaum 65/66 F5
Rosenblatt.... 67/68 C13
Rothschild, Sderot ....
65/66 D-E 7-8
Rovigo............67/68 E11
Rovina 63/64 F2
Ruhama 67/68 C11
Ruppin.......65/66 D5-6
Russian 67/68 B11
Ruth 65/66 E6
Saadiah Gaon.. 65/66 F8
Salsila 67/68 B13
Salvador 63/64 G1
Samuel Ben Adaya ....
67/68 A12-13
Sanhedrin.... 63/64 G2-3
Sapir............. 65/66 E7
Sarid............. 67/68 A13
Schlesinger 63/64 G3
Schmerling... 67/68 C10

Schnitzler 67/68 C11
Schocken 67/68 E11
Schorr, Moshe 63/64 F4
Segev......67/68 A11-12
Seifan 67/68 B13
Sgula 67/68 C10-11
Sha'ar Tzion ... 63/64 D3
Sha'arei Nicanor...........
67/68 A-B12
Sha'arei Tshuva ....
67/68 E11
Shabazi67/68 C-D 9-10
Shadal 67/68 E9
Shalag 65/66 C-D6
Shalom Aleichem ....
65/66 D6-7
Shapira 65/66 E7
Sharabi 67/68 D9-10
Sharett, Moshe............
63/64 F-G 4-5
Shatz 65/66 D5
Shaul Hamelech, Sderot .
65/66 F-G 6-7
Shaviv 67/68 B13
She'erit Yisra'el.............
67/68 C11
Shefer.............67/68 D9
Shefer, Simta..............
65/66 D8-9
Sheinkin 65/66 E8
Shenkar 67/68 C9
Sherira Gaon..................
67/68 C-D12
Sherira, Simta ....
67/68 D12
Shilo 65/66 F6
Shimon Hatarsi63/64 E3
Shimon Hatzadik...........
67/68 B11
Shimoni, David..............
63/64 G1
Shimshon Hagibor ....
65/66 E6-7
Shir 65/66 D5
Shivtei Yisra'el..............
67/68 B12-13
Shlabim . 67/68 D11-12
Shlomo Hamelech ....
65/66 E5-7
Shlomo, Derech ....
67/68 C-E11
Shlomtzion Hamalka ......
63/64 F3
Shloshet Hahitzim..........
67/68 E13
Shmaya 67/68 B11
Shmuel Hanagid.............
65/66 E5
Shneour, Zalman ....
65/66 D7
Shnitzler 67/68 C11
Shor, Aryeh .. 67/68 B11
Shulamit 65/66 E6
Smilansky 63/64 G4
Smolenskin..... 65/66 D6
Smuts, Sderot ....
63/64 F3-4
Sokolow, Nahum.............
63/64 E3-4
Soncino............ 65/66 G8
Soutine, Chaim ....
65/66 F5-6
Spinoza............ 65/66 E6
Sprinzak 65/66 F7
Stand................ 65/66 E6
Stein 67/68 D10
Stern...............67/68 D10

Straus.............65/66 D8
Stricker 63/64 F3-4
Struck 65/66 E5
Stybel 65/66 G8
Syrkin 65/66 D6-7
Tahkemoni 67/68 D9
Tahon.............. 63/64 D4
Tajar, Tziona 67/68 B12
Tanhum........ 67/68 B11
Tapu'ah .. 67/68 B12-13
Tarmav 65/66 C8
Tarsat, Sderot.. 65/66 E7
Tartzav 67/68 C9
Tashah 65/66 F5
Tayelet Mifratz Shlomo ..
67/68 B11
Tchernichowsky.............
65/66 D7
Tchlenov........67/68 E10
Tel Hai 65/66 E7
Tiomkin 65/66 E9
Tirtza 67/68 C11
Toscanini 65/66 F7
Trumpeldor.... 65/66 D7
Tut 67/68 B13
Tuvya Harofeh................
67/68 B13
Tverya 65/66 D7
Tzahalon Harofeh ....
67/68 B13
Tzfat................ 65/66 D7
Tzidon............. 63/64 D3
Tzihatli 67/68 B-C13
Tzofit............. 67/68 A13
Tzrifin...........67/68 D10
Uri 65/66 F6
Uriel da Costa ....
67/68 D10
Ussishkin 63/64 E3
Vakhtangov.. 67/68 C13
Ve'idat Kattowitz............
63/64 G3
Vilna 65/66 D5
Vital 67/68 D10-11
Vitale, Maurizio ....
63/64 F2
Vitkin 63/64 D4
Vormaiza......... 65/66 E5
Warburg 65/66 E7
Washington, Sderot ....
67/68 D10-11
Wasserman, Ya'akov ......
67/68 C11
Weiner 67/68 B12
Weisel............. 65/66 E5
Weiss 65/66 D5
Weizmann, Chaim..........
63/64 G5-6
Wilson 65/66 F8
Wissotzky...... 63/64 G4
Wolffsohn 67/68 D-E10
Ya'ari 63/64 E-F2
Ya'el 65/66 E6
Yabez 67/68 D9
Yaffe, Bezalel .. 67/68 E9
Yafo, Derech 67/68 D10
Yakiniton........ 67/68 C9
Yalag 65/66 E6
Yarhinay, Shmuel ....
67/68 B13
Yavne'el.......... 67/68 D9
Yavneh 67/68 E9
Yefeh Nof 63/64 D4
Yefet........67/68 B11-12
Yehalel 65/66 E5

Yehezkel 63/64 D-E 3-4
Yehi'eli.........67/68 C10
Yeho'ash 65/66 D6
Yehoshua Bin Nun ....
63/64 E3-5
Yehuda Halevi ....
65/66 D-F 8-10
Yehuda Hamaccabi........
63/64 F-G3
Yehuda Hayamit ....
67/68 B12
Yehuda Hehasid ....
67/68 D9
Yehuda Meragusa...........
67/68 B11-12
Yellin, David ... 63/64 F4
Yeriho...............63/64 E4
Yerushalayim, Sderot......
67/68 B-C 12-13
Yeshayahu....... 63/64 E3
Yeshivat Volozhin ....
67/68 C10
Yeshurun.... 65/66 D5-6
Yihye............... 65/66 D8
Yirmiyahu 63/64 D3
Yishkon 65/66 D8
Yisra'els 65/66 D6
Yitzhak Sadeh63/64 F-G
8-9
Yo'ezer 67/68 B11
Yodfat 65/66 D5
Yoel 63/64 E3
Yo'ezer 67/68 B11
Yohanan Hagadi ....
63/64 F3
Yohanan Hasandlar ....
65/66 D8
Yohanan Hyrcanus ....
63/64 E3
Yom Tov 65/66 D8
Yona Hanavi ....
65/66 C-D8
Yonatan Havafsi ....
63/64 F3
Yose Ben Yose67/68 B-C
11-12
Yosef Eliyahu .. 65/66 E7
Yosef Hanasi ... 65/66 E8
Yotzer, Sderot . 63/64 E4
Yust 65/66 D5
Zadok Hakohen...............
65/66 D8-9
Zamenhof....65/66 E6-7
Zangwill..... 63/64 D-E4
Zangwill, Simta ....
63/64 D-E4
Zatori 63/64 G3
Zechariah....... 63/64 D3
Zeitlin 65/66 F6
Zephaniah..... 63/64 D3
Zerubavel...... 65/66 C8
Zevulun.......67/68 E10
Zichron Ya'akov..............
65/66 G5
Ziklag 65/66 F8
Zirelson, Harav.................
63/64 G3
Ziv, Rivka 65/66 F6
Zlatopolsky 65/66 D5
Zola, Emile . 65/66 D5-6
Zunz 67/68 D13
668 .... 65/66 F6
734 ....63/64 E3
1098 .... 65/66 F6
1217 .... 65/66 F9
1246 .... 65/66 F9

1274 .... 65/66 F9
1275 .... 65/66 F9
1276 .... 65/66 F9
1277 .... 65/66 F9
1278 .... 65/66 F9
1284 ....63/64 E3
2007 .... 63/64 G1
2604 ....67/68 E13
3043 .... 67/68 B12
3048 ......67/68 B11-12
3052 ...... 67/68 B12
3053 ...... 67/68 B12
3055 ...... 67/68 B12
3057 ...... 67/68 B12
3070 ...... 67/68 C12
3071 ...... 67/68 C12
3083 ...... 67/68 A12
3088 ...... 67/68 A12
3090 ...... 67/68 A12
3092 ...... 67/68 A12
3094 ...... 67/68 A12
3102 ...... 67/68 A13
3182 ......67/68 C12-13
3210 ...... 67/68 B13
3211 ...... 67/68 B13
3280 .... 67/68 B-C10
3288 ...... 67/68 B11
3312 ...... 67/68 C11
3313 ...... 67/68 C11
3318 ...... 67/68 C11
3320 ...... 67/68 C12
3321 ...... 67/68 B-C11
3323 ...... 67/68 C11
3335 ...... 67/68 C12
3350 ...... 67/68 B11
3351 ...... 67/68 B11
3357 ...... 67/68 C10
3358 ...... 67/68 C10
3359 ...... 67/68 C10
3361 ......67/68 D10
3363 ......67/68 D10
3377 ......67/68 E12
3378 ...... 67/68 D12
3380 ...... 67/68 B11
3381 ...... 67/68 D12
3382 ......67/68 D13
3383 ......67/68 E12
3431 ...... 67/68 D12-13
3443 ...... 67/68 B12
3731 ...... 67/68 A12
3732 ...... 67/68 B12
3733 ...... 67/68 B12
3735 .... 67/68 B11-12
3737 ...... 67/68 B12
3738 ...... 67/68 B12
3739 ...... 67/68 B12
3741 ...... 67/68 A12
3742 ...... 67/68 A12
3744 ...... 67/68 B12
3750 ......67/68 A12-13
3768 ...... 67/68 B13
3783 ......67/68 D-E12
3784 ......67/68 D-E12
3785 ......67/68 D-E12
3789 ......67/68 E11
3812 ......67/68 D10
3831 ......67/68 D13
3838 ......67/68 D12
3844 ...... 67/68 B12
3887 ...... 67/68 A12
3888 ...... 67/68 A12
3890 ...... 67/68 A12

A

Abasan el Kabir 35 A14
Abdeh 31 E13
Abdin 4 G4
Abdullah Bridge (defunct) 18 G10
Abirim 8 D3
Abud 19 D9
Abu Dis 17 F11
Abu Ghosh 20 E11
Abu Qash 20 E10
Abu Qureinat 39 E15
Abu Shukheidim 20 E10
Abu Sinan 7 D4
Abwein 20 E9
Achziv 7 C3
Adam - see Geva Benyamin
Adamit 8 D3
Adanim 22 C9
Adeisa 1 E1
Aderet 25 D12
Adi 8 D5
Adirim 9 E6
Adora 25 E12
Afek 7 C4
Afek Industrial Park 22 D9
Afik 4 G4
Afikim 10 F5
Afula 9 E6
Afula Ilit 9 E5
Agam Montfort 8 D3
Agur 25 D12
Ahi'ezer 22 C10
Ahihud 8 D4
Ahisamach 22 C10
Ahituv 15 C7
Ahuzam 28 C13
Ahuzat Barak 9 E5
Ahuzat Naftali 6 E4
Ahva 28 C11
Air Force Museum 33 C15
Ajeh 16 D7
Ajul 20 E9
Akbara 6 E3
Akko (Acre) 7 C4
Akko Station 7 C4
Alei Zahav 19 D9
Alfei Menashe 16 D9
Allenby Border Crossing - see King Husein Bridge
Allon Road 15-18 F7-10
Alma 1 E3
'Alma esh Sha'b 7 C3
Almagor 3 F3
Almog 18 G10
Almon (Anatot) 17 F10
Alon 17 F10
Alonei Abba 12 D5
Alonei Habashan 2 G2
Alonei Mamreh 23 E12
Alonei Yitzhak 11 C6

Alon Hagalil 12 D5
Alonim 12 D5
Alon Shvut 23 E12
Alon Tavor Field School 9 E5
Aluma 28 C12
Alumim 36 B14
Alumot 10 F5
Amatzya 25 D13
Ami'ad 6 E3
Amikam 11 C6
Aminadav 23 E11
Ami'oz 44 B15
Amir 1 F2
Amirim 5 E3
Amka 7 D3
Ammonites' Wall 48 E18
Amnon 3 F3
Amram's Pillars 58 G24
Amuka 6 E3
Amuriya 20 E9
Anabta 16 D8
Anata 17 F10
Ancient Dor 11 C6
Ancient Korazim Nat. Park 3 F3
Andartat Habik'a (Memorial) 14 F9
Andartat Oz 77 (Memorial) 2 G1
Ani'am 4 G3
Anin 12 D6
Anzeh 13 E7
Aqaba 58 G25
Aqaba Airport 58 G24
Aqabeh 13 E7
Aqbat Jabar (Refugee Camp) 18 F10
Aqrabeh 13 F8
Ara 12 D6
Araba 5 E4
Arabeh 16 D7
Arab el Mashra 10 F6
Arab es Sawahra 17 F11
Arab Shibli 9 E5
Arabuneh 9 E6
Arad 29 F14
Arad Phosphate Factory 37 F15
Aramsha 8 D3
Araneh 9 E6
Araqa 12 D7
Ar'ara 12 D6
Ar'ara Banegev 39 E15
Arava 58 G23-24
Arava Border Crossing 58 G24
Arbel 6 E4
Argaman 14 F8
Ari'el 20 E9
Artas 23 E11
Arugot 28 C11
Arura 20 E9
Arvat Sedom 38 G16
Arvat Yafruk 52 G21

Arvot Hayarden 18 G10
Aseret 27 C11
Asfar (Meitzad) 23 E12
Ashalim 42 D16
Ashalim Beach 3 F4
Ashdod 27 B11
Ashdod Port (Nemal Ashdod) 27 B11
Ashdot Ya'akov (Ihud) 10 F5
Ashdot Ya'akov (Me'uhad) 10 F5
Ashkelon 27 B12
Asira el Qibliyeh 13 E8
Asira esh Shamaliyeh 13 E8
Askar 13 E8
Atara 20 E9
Atarot Airport 20 E10
Atar Utzbat Barak (Memorial) 2 F2
Atawna 34 D14
Ateret 20 E9
Atil 16 D7
Atlit 11 C5
Atlit Station 11 C5
Avdon 7 C3
Avi'el 11 C6
Avi'ezer 25 D12
Avigdor 28 C12
Avihayil 15 C9
Avital 9 E6
Avivim 1 E2
Avnat 24 G11
Avnei Eitan 4 G4
Avnei Hefetz 16 D8
Avshalom 43 A15
Avtalyon 5 E4
Awarta 13 E8
Ayanot 21 C10
Ayelet Hashahar 1 F3
Azarya 22 D10
Azmut 13 E8
Azor 21 C10
Azri'el 15 C9
Azrikam 27 C11
Azun 16 D8
Azun Atmeh 19 D9

B

Ba'al Hatzor 20 E9
Bahan 15 D7
Bal'aa 16 D7
Balata 13 E8
Balfouriya 9 E5
Banias 2 F1
Bani Na'im 23 E12
Bani Suheila 35 A14
Baqa 16 D8
Baqa el Gharbiya 16 D7
Baqa esh Sharqiya 16 D7
Baqura 10 F5
Barak 9 E6
Bar'am 1 E3
Bardaleh 14 F7
Bareket 22 D10

Bar Giyora 25 E11
Barka'i 12 C7
Barkan 16 D9
Barta'a 12 D7
Bar Yehuda Landing Strip 2 G13
Bar Yohai 5 E3
Basmat Tab'un 12 D5
Bat Ayin 26 E12
Bat Galim Station 11 C5
Bat Hadar 27 B12
Bat Hefer 15 D8
Bat Shlomo 11 C6
Bat Yam 21 C10
Batzra 15 C9
Bazariya 16 D8
Bedouin Heritage Center 33 C14
Be'er Ada 51 F20
Be'er Ef'eh 29 F15
Be'er Hadaj 42 D16
Be'er Hafir 4 C18
Be'er Hayil 42 D16
Be'eri 36 B14
Be'eri Hayeshana (Old Be'eri) 36 B14
Be'er Karkom 54 E20
Be'er Mash'abim 42 D16
Be'er Menuha 52 G20
Be'er Milhan 56 F23
Be'er Milka 44 B17
Be'er Ora 58 G24
Be'erot Aro'er 39 E15
Be'erotayim 15 C9
Be'erot Oded 54 D19
Be'erot Yitzhak 22 C9
Be'er Ratav 37 F16
Be'er Resisim 50 C18
Beersheba (Be'er Sheva) 34 D14
Be'er Sheva 34 D14
Be'er Toviya 27 C12
Be'er Ya'akov 22 C10
Be'er Ya'akov Station 22 C10
Be'er Zahal 39 D15
Begin Tzafon 20 E10
Beita 13 E8
Beit Aahronsohn 11 C6
Beit Alfa 10 F5
Beit Amin 16 D9
Beitanya Ilit 10 F5
Beitar 23 E11
Beit Araa 4 G4
Beit Ari'eh 19 D9
Beit Arif 22 D10
Beitar Ilit 23 E11
Beit Awa 25 D13
Beit Awla 25 E12
Beit Berl 15 C9
Beit Dagan 22 C10
Beit Dajan 14 F8
Beit Dubrovin 1 F2
Beit Duqu 20 E10
Beit El 20 E10

Beit El'azari 22 C11
Beit er Rosh el Fawqa ...
34 D13
Beit er Rosh et Tahta ....
34 D13
Beit Eshel 34 D15
Beit Ezra 27 B12
Beit Fajar 23 E12
Beit Furik 13 E8
Beit Gamli'el 21 C11
Beit Gavri'el 3 F5
Beit Ghur el Fawqa
(Upper Beit Horon) ......
20 E10
Beit Ghur et Tahta
(Lower Beit Horon) ......
19 D10
Beit Guvrin 25 D12
Beit Ha'arava 18 G10
Beit Ha'emek 7 C3
Beit Hagadi 33 C14
Beit Halevi 15 C9
Beit Halord 15 C8
Beit Hameches
Ha'elyon 2 F3
Beit Hanan 21 C10
Beit Hananya 11 C6
Beit Hanina 20 E10
Beit Hanun 36 B13
Beit Hashita 10 E6
Beit Hashmonai 22 D10
Beit Herut 15 C7
Beit Herzl 22 D11
Beit Hilkiya 28 C11
Beit Hillel 1 E2
Beit Iba 13 E8
Beit Ijza 20 E10
Beit Iksa 20 E11
Beitilu 19 E10
Beitin 20 E10
Beit I'nan 20 E10
Beit Jala 23 E11
Beit Jan 5 E3
Beit Jimal 25 D11
Beit Kahil 26 E12
Beit Kama 33 C13
Beit Keshet 9 E5
Beit Lahiyeh 36 B13
Beit Lehem Haglilit ......
12 D5
Beit Lid 16 D8
Beit Liqya 19 D10
Beit Me'ir 19 D11
Beit Mirsim 34 D13
Beit Nehemya ... 22 D10
Beit Nekofa 20 E11
Beit Nir 25 D12
Beit Oren 11 C5
Beit Oved 21 C10
Beit Qad 9 E6
Beit Rabban 27 C11
Beit Rima 19 D9
Beit Rimon 5 E4
Beit Rishonim 21 B10
Beit Sahur 23 E11
Beit Saida 3 F3
Beit Saida Valley 3 F3
Beit She'an 10 F6
Beit She'arim 12 D5
Beit Shemesh 25 D11
Beit Shemesh Station ......
25 D11
Beit Shikma 27 B12
Beit Sira 19 D10
Beit Surik 20 E11

Beit Tzur 26 E12
Beit Tzvi 11 C5
Beit Umar 23 E12
Beit Umrin 13 E8
Beituniya 20 E10
Beitunya 20 E10
Beit Uzi'el 22 D11
Beit Wazan 13 E8
Beit Yanai 15 C7
Beit Yehoshua 15 C9
Beit Yehoshua Station ..
15 C9
Beit Yitzhak Sha'ar
Hefer 15 C9
Beit Yosef 10 F6
Beit Zaid 12 D5
Beit Zayit 20 E11
Beit Zera 10 F5
Beka'ot 14 F8
Beko'a 22 D11
Ben Ami 7 C3
Benaya 21 C11
Ben Gurion Airport ......
22 C10
Ben Gurion Park 3 E15
Ben Gurion's Grave
National Park .. 47 D17
Ben Gurion's Hut ......
47 D17
Ben Gurion University .
34 D14
Ben Shemen (Youth
Village) 22 D10
Ben Shemen 22 C10
Ben Zakai 21 C11
Berechya 27 B12
Bethlehem (Beit
Lehem) 23 E11
Betzet 7 C3
Bidu 20 E10
Bidya 19 D9
Bik'at Arad 29 E-F14
Bik'at Ardon 45 F18
Bik'at Beit Hakerem
5 D4
Bik'at Beit Netofa ......
5 D-E4
Bik'at Hatil 34 D14
Bik'at Hayarden Field
School 14 F9
Bik'at Hayare'ah 57 F24
Bik'at Hisun 53 D20
Bik'at Hurkanya 18 F11
Bik'at Kana'im ......
29 F13-14
Bik'at Ketura 56 G21
Bik'at Ksulot 9 E5
Bik'at Mahmal ... 48 E18
Bik'at Na'atzutz . 56 F22
Bik'atr Tir'an 5 E5
Bik'at Sanur 13 E7
Bik'at Sayarim ... 55 F23
Bik'at Sichnin 5 D4
Bik'at Timna 58 G23
Bik'at Tzehiha ......
52-53 F20-21
Bik'at Tzenifim 55
E-F21-22
Bik'at Tzin 48 E17
Bik'at Tzva'im ... 37 F15
Bik'at Uvda 56 F22
Bik'at Yaval 34 D13
Bik'at Yavne'el 3 F5
Bikura 10 F6
Bil'in 19 D10
Bi'na 5 D4

Bint Jubail 1 E2
Binyamina 11 C6
Binyamina Station ......
11 C7
Biq'at Kedesh 1 E2
Biranit 8 D3
Bir Asluj 42 D16
Bir el Ma'in 53 D20
Bir el Maksur 8 D5
Bir es Sika 16 D7
Biriya 6 E3
Bir Nabala 20 E10
Bir Zeit 20 E10
Bitan Aharon 15 C9
Bitanya Ilit 3 F5
Bit'ha 33 C14
Bitzaron 27 C11
Blida 1 E2
Bnei Atarot 22 C10
Bnei Ayish 28 C11
Bnei Brak 21 C9
Bnei Brak Station 21 C9
Bnei Darom 27 C11
Bnei Dror 15 C9
Bnei Re'em 28 C11
Bnei Tziyon 15 C9
Bnei Yehuda 4 F4
Bnot Ya'akov Bridge ......
2 F3
Bor Mashash 39 D15
Borot Haketzinim ......
48 E18
Borot Lotz 53 D19
Bracha 13 E8
Breichat Haktzinim ......
3 F3
Breichat Hameshushim
3 F3
Breichat Man 2 F1
Breichat Meshushei
Zavitan 3 F3
Breichat Na'ama ......
29 F13
Breichat Ram 2 F1
Breichat Tzefira 29 F13
Breichat Ya'ar 15 C7
Bror Hayil 33 C13
Brosh 33 C14
Bruchin 19 D9
Brurim 28 C11
Bu'eina-Nujeidat .. 5 E4
Bukei'a (Peki'in) .. 8 D3
Buqata 2 F1
Burgeta 15 C9
Burham 20 E10
Burin 13 E8
Burj Beitin (Beit El) ......
20 E10
Burj el Malih 14 F7
Burqa (Samaria) . 13 E8
Burqa (Judea) 20 E10
Burqin 9 E7
Buruqin 19 D9
Bustan Hagalil 7 C4

C

Caesarea 11 C7
Caesarea -Pardes Hana
Station 11 C7
Capernaum - see Gan
Le'umi Kfar Nahum
Canada Park .. 19 D11
Carmel Field School
11 C5
Central Haifa Station ......
11 C5

Central Tel Aviv Station
21 C9
Church of the Bread
and Fishes 3 F4

D

Daburiya 9 E5
Dafna 1 F1
Daheisheh 23 E11
Daliya 12 D6
Daliyat el Karmil 11 C5
Dalton 6 E3
Dan 1 F1
Danaba 16 D8
Dangur Memorial ......
43 A15
Dead Sea 18 G11
Deganya A 3 F5
Deganya B 3 F5
Deir Abu Da'if 9 E6
Deir Abu Mash'al ......
19 D10
Deir Amar 19 D10
Deir Balut 19 D9
Deir Cremisan ... 23 E11
Deir Dibwan 20 E10
Deir el Asad 5 D4
Deir el Asal el Fawqa ....
34 D13
Deir el Asal et Tahta ......
34 D13
Deir el Balah 35 A14
Deir el Ghusun 16 D7
Deir el Hatab 13 E8
Deir el Qarantal 18 F10
Deir es Sudan 20 E9
Deir Ghasaneh ... 19 D9
Deir Ghazaleh 9 E6
Deir Hajla 18 G10
Deir Hana 5 E4
Deir Ibzi' 20 E10
Deir Istiya 16 D9
Deir Jarir 17 F10
Deir Krukh 4 G3
Deir Mar Jiryas
(Monastery of St.
George) 18 F10
Deir Nizam 19 E9
Deir Qadis 19 D10
Deir Razikh 31 E13
Deir Samit 25 D13
Deir Sharaf 13 E8
Deir Sirin 1 E1
Dekel 43 A15
Derech Burma .. 19 D11
Derech Habesamim
(Perfume Route) ......
45 F18
Derech Habesamim
(Perfume Route) ......
46 F18
Derech Haneft .. 42 D16
Derech Hapesalim ......
25 D11
Derech Hayarden
Haharari 3 F3
Desert Sculpture Park .
48 E18
Dimona 39 E15
Dishon 1 E2
Dolev 20 E10
Dolmens 4 G3
Dor 11 C6
Dorot 33 C13
Dovev 5 E3
Dovrat 9 E5

Duda'im (Refuse
disposal site) 33 C14
Duma (Jordan Valley) ..
17 F9
Duma (Judea) ... 31 E13
Dura (Adora'im) ....
26 E13
Dura el Qari' 20 E10
Dvira 34 D13
Dvora 9 E6
E
Ed Dahi 9 E5
Ed Dumeida 5 D4
Efrata (Efrat) ... 23 E12
Egyptian Army
Memorial 27 C12
Eilabun 5 E4
Eilat 58 G25
Eilat Airport 58 G25
Eilat Border Crossing
(Taba) 58 G25
Eilat Field School ....
58 G25
Eilon 8 D3
Eilon Moreh 13 E8
Eilot 58 G24
Einabus 13 E8
Ein Akev 47 D17
Ein Akrabim ... 37 F16
Ein Amatzyahu 38 G16
Ein Amud 6 E4
Ein Ardon 48 E18
Ein Arik 20 E10
Einat 22 C9
Einav 16 D8
Ein Avdat 47 D17
Ein Ayala 11 C6
Ein Bokek 2 G14
Ein Carmel 11 C5
Ein Dor 9 E5
Ein Duyuk 18 F10
Ein el Asad 5 E3
Ein el Awja 17 F9
Ein el Fari'a 13 E7
Ein el Fuwar ... 17 F10
Ein el Hufeira ... 46 G17
Ein el Maqura 11 C6
Ein es Sahla 12 D6
Ein Evrona 58 G24
Ein Farod 5 E3
Ein Fit 2 F1
Ein Gedi 24 G13
Ein Gedi Baths ... 2 G13
Ein Gedi Field School .....
24 G12
Ein Gev 3 F4
Ein Habesor 36 B15
Ein Hadayig 1 F2
Ein Ha'emek 12 D6
Ein Hahoresh ... 15 C7
Ein Hame'ara ... 53 D20
Ein Hamifratz ... 7 C4
Ein Hanatziv 10 F6
Ein Harod (Ihud) ... 9 E6
Ein Harod (Me'uhad) ....
9 E6
Ein Hashlosha ... 35 B14
Ein Hashofet 12 D6
Ein Hatzeva 38 G17
Ein Hatzeva Field
School 46 G17
Ein Hemed 20 E11
Ein Hod 11 C5
Ein Hur 1 E2
Ein Ibrahim 12 D6

Ein Iron 11 C7
Ein Kamonim 5 E4
Ein Kerem Agric.
School 20 E11
Ein Ketura 56 G22
Ein Kunya 2 F1
Ein Mabu'a 17 F10
Ein Mahil 9 E5
Ein Mashak 46 F17
Ein Mor 47 D17
Ein Namer 2 F13
Ein Naquba 20 E11
Ein Netafim 58 F24
Ein Ofarim 38 G16
Ein Orahot 45 F17
Einot Dekalim ... 25 D11
Einot Einan 1 E2
Einot Kaneh 24 G11
Einot Petza'el 17 F9
Einot Tzipori ... 12 D5
Einot Tzukim (Ein
Fash'ha) 18 G11
Ein Prat 17 F10
Ein Qelt 18 F10
Ein Qini 12 D6
Ein Qiniya 20 E10
Ein Qudeirat 49 C19
Ein Rafa 20 E11
Ein Rahel 46 G18
Ein Saharonim ... 48 E18
Ein Samiyeh 17 F9
Ein Sarid 15 C9
Ein Sharuhen ... 36 B15
Ein Shaviv 48 E17
Ein Shemer 15 C7
Ein Sheva (Tabgha) ....
3 F4
Ein Siniya 20 E10
Ein Tamar 38 G16
Ein Tamir 8 D3
Ein Tzalmon 5 E4
Ein Tze'elim 2 G13
Ein Tzin 37 F16
Ein Tzurim 27 C12
Ein Vered 15 C9
Ein Ya'akov 8 D3
Ein Yabrud 20 E10
Ein Ya'el 23 E11
Ein Yahav 46 G18
Ein Yorke'am ... 37 F16
Ein Yotvata 56 G22
Ein Zeitim 6 E3
Ein Zeved 5 E3
Ein Zik 48 E17
Ein Ziv 8 D3
Ein Zivan 2 G2
Eitan 28 C13
Eitanim 20 E11
Eitarun 1 E2
El'ad 22 D9
El Adasiya 10 F5
El Amin 3 F3
El Atara 16 D7
El Atatra 36 B13
El'azar 23 E12
El Bahja (Bahai
Temple) 7 C4
El Bayada 12 D6
El Bira 20 E10
El Buqei'a 14 F8
El Bureij 35 A14
El Burj 34 D13
El Eizariyeh 17 F11
El Fandaqumiyeh 13 E7

El Fasayil (Phasaelis) .....
18 F9
El Fawar 31 E13
El Funduq 16 D8
El Hajira 26 E13
El Hashimiyeh 12 D7
El Heima 10 F6
El Huzayil 33 C14
Eli 20 E9
Eli Ad 4 G4
Elifaz 58 G23
Elifelet 3 F3
Elishama 15 C9
El Jab'a 26 E12
El Jib 20 E10
Elkana 19 D9
El Khadab 31 E13
El Khadr 23 E11
El Khiyam 1 E1
Elkosh 8 D3
El Luban 19 D9
El Majid 34 D13
El Manshiya 10 F5
El Mashri 10 F6
El Mazra'a el Qibliya .....
20 E10
El Mazra'a esh
Sharqiyeh 20 E9
El Midyeh 19 D10
El Mughayir (Samaria) ...
9 E7
El Mughayir (Judea) ......
17 F9
El Mughazi 35 A14
El Mukhayba 4 G5
El Musheirifa ... 12 D6
El Qubeibeh ... 20 E10
El Rom 2 F1
Elyachin 15 C7
Elyakim 11 C6
El Yamun 9 D6
El Yarmuk 4 G4
Elyashiv 15 C7
Emaus Church ... 20 E10
Emek Ayalon 19
D10-11
Emek Dotan 9 E7
Emek Ha'ela 25
D11-12
Emek Hamichmetat ....
13 E8
Emek Harod 9 E6
Emek Hefer 15 C7
Emek Maharal ... 11 C6
Emek Yizre'el ... 12 D6
Emek Zohar 2 G15
Emek Zvulun 7 C4
Emunim 27 C12
Engineers Corps
Memorial 22 D11
En Nabi Hizqin ... 13 E7
En Nabi Musa ... 18 F10
En Nabi Rubin ... 13 E7
En Nabi Salih 19 E9
En Naqura 13 E8
En Nazla el Gharbiya ....
16 D7
En Nazla el Wusta ....
16 D7
En Nazla esh Sharqiya .
16 D7
Eretz Breishit ... 17 F10
Erez 36 B13
Er Ram 20 E10
Er Rameh 16 D7
Er Ras 16 D8

Er Rihiya 31 E13
Eshbal 5 D4
Eshbol 33 C13
Eshel Avraham ... 23 E12
Eshel Hanasi ... 33 C14
Esh'har 5 D4
Eshkolot 34 D13
Esh Shuna 10 F5
Esh Shuyukh ... 23 E12
Eshta'ol 19 D11
Es Samu'a 31 E13
Es Sawiyeh 20 E9
Et Tayiba 16 D8
Et Tayibeh 17 F10
Et Tel (Ai) 20 E10
Et Tira 20 E10
Etz Efra'im 19 D9
Etziyon Gever ... 58 G25
Even Menahem 8 D3
Even Sapir 20 E11
Even Shmu'el ... 28 C12
Even Yehuda ... 15 C9
Evron 7 C3
Eyal 15 C9
Ezer 27 C12
Ezuz 49 C18
Ez Zababideh ... 13 E7
Ez Zahariyeh ... 31 E13
Ez Za'im 17 F11
Ez Zawiyeh 19 D9
F
Fahmeh 16 D7
Falama 16 D8
Faqu'a 9 E6
Far'a el Jiftlik ... 14 F8
Far'ata 13 E8
Farkha 20 E9
Farod 5 E3
Far'un 16 D8
Fasuta 8 D3
Firasin 16 D7
Fureidis 11 C6
G
Ga'ash 15 C9
Ga'aton 8 D3
Gadish 12 D6
Gadot 1 F3
Gai Shani (The Red
Canyon) 57 F24
Gai Shayarot ... 19 D11
Gal'ed (Even Yitzhak) ..
12 D6
Galilee 5 D-E4
Galilee Beduin
Museum 9 E5
Gal'on 25 D12
Galya 21 C11
Gamla 4 G3
Ganei'am 22 C9
Ganei Hadar ... 22 C11
Ganei Hadar (Mizrah) .
22 C11
Ganei Huga 10 F6
Ganei Tikva 22 C9
Ganei Yehoshu'a (Park
Hayarkon) 21 C9
Ganei Yehuda ... 22 C9
Ganei Yohanan 22 C11
Gan Hadarom ... 27 C11
Gan Hayim 15 C9
Gan Le'umi Achziv ....
7 C3
Gan Le'umi Ashkelon ....
27 B12

Gan Le'umi Avdat 47 D17
Gan Le'umi Beit Alfa
(Anc. Syn.) 10 E6
Gan Le'umi Beit
Guvrin-Maresha ....
25 D12
Gan Le'umi Beit She'an
10 F6
Gan Le'umi Beit
She'arim 12 D5
Gan Le'umi Ben Gurion
(Grave) 47 D17
Gan Le'umi Caesarea ....
11 C7
Gan Le'umi Carmel ....
11 C5
Gan Le'umi Ein Avdat ..
47 D17
Gan Le'umi Gan
Hashlosha (Sahneh) .....
10 F6
Gan Le'umi Habesor
(Eshkol) 36 B15
Gan Le'umi Hamat
Tverya 3 F4
Gan Le'umi Herodion
(Har Hordus) 23 F11
Gan Le'umi Homot
Ha'ir Ha'atika .. 20 E11
Gan Le'umi Horshat Tal
21 F1
Gan Le'umi Horvot
Shivta 4 C17
Gan Le'umi Kfar
Bar'am 5 E3
Gan Le'umi Kfar
Nahum 3 F4
Gan Le'umi Kochav
Hayarden (Belvoir) .....
10 F5
Gan Le'umi Kursi . 3 F4
Gan Le'umi Ma'ayan
Harod 9 E6
Gan Le'umi Mamshit ...
3 E16
Gan Le'umi Metzada ...
2 G13
Gan Le'umi Metzudat
Nimrod 2 F1
Gan Le'umi Migdal
Afek 22 D9
Gan Le'umi Mivtzar
Yehi'am 8 D3
Gan Le'umi Nahal
Alexander 15 C7
Gan Le'umi Nahal
Tzalmon 5 E4
Gan Le'umi Park
Hasharon 15 C7
Gan Le'umi Qumran ....
18 G11
Gan Le'umi Shomron
(Sebastiya) 13 E8
Gan Le'umi Tel Arad
29 F14
Gan Le'umi Tel Be'er
Sheva 34 D14
Gan Le'umi Tel Hatzor
1 E3
Gan Le'umi Tel
Megiddo 12 D6
Gan Le'umi Tzipori ....
5 D5
Gan Le'umi Yad
Mordechai 27 B13
Gan Ner 9 E6
Ganot 21 C10
Ganot Hadar 15 C9

Gan Shlomo 21 C11
Gan Shmu'el 15 C7
Gan Shomron 15 C7
Gan Sorek 21 C10
Gan Yavneh 27 C11
Gan Yoshiya 15 C7
Gat 28 C12
Gat Rimon 22 C9
Gaza (Aza) 36-37 A13
Gaza Strip .. 35 A13-14
Gazit 10 E5
Ge'a 27 B12
Gebel el Hamra .. 57 F24
Gebel er Risha .. 49 C18
Gebel es Safra .. 57 F24
Gebel Qurein Atud ....
57 F24
Gebel Suweiqa .. 57 E23
Gebel Umm Haluf ....
53 D21
Gedera 28 C11
Gedud 51 Memorial .....
27 C12
Gefen 25 D11
Gelil Yam 21 C9
Gesher 10 F5
Gesher Adam (Damiya)
14 G8
Gesher Ad Halom ....
27 B11
Gesher Arik 3 F3
Gesher Bnot Ya'akov ..
3 F3
Gesher Hayeshana ....
10 F5
Gesher Haziv 7 C3
Gesher Nahara'im ....
10 F5
Gesher Paz 11 C5
Geshur 4 G4
Ge'ulei Teiman ... 15 C7
Ge'ulim 15 C9
Geva 9 E6
Geva Benyamin
(Adam) 17 F10
Geva Carmel 11 C6
Gevim 36 B13
Gezer 22 D10
Ghajar 1 E1
Ghor el Far'ia 14 F8
Gid'ona 9 E6
Gil'am 7 D4
Gilat 33 C14
Gilgal 18 F9
Gilon 8 D4
Gimzo 22 D10
Ginaton 22 C10
Gineigar 12 D5
Ginosar 6 E4
Ginosar Valley 6 E4
Ginot Shomron ... 16 D8
Gita 8 D3
Gitit 14 F9
Giv'a 69 .... 27 B12
Giv'at Ada 11 C6
Giv'at Agudal ... 51 E19
Giv'at Amram .. 58 G24
Giv'at Avni 6 E4
Giv'atayim 21 C9
Giv'at Bahat 58 G24
Giv'at Bazak 4 G3
Giv'at Brenner .. 22 C11
Giv'at Ela 12 D5
Giv'at Hablanim ....
42 D15

Giv'at Hakrav ....
25 E11-12
Giv'at Haminzar ....
23 E12
Giv'at Hamoreh ... 9 E5
Giv'at Hanun Dalet ....
18 F10
Giv'at Harut 48 E18
Giv'at Hashlosha 22 C9
Giv'at Haviva 15 C7
Giv'at Hayil 42 D16
Givat Hayim (Ihud) ......
16 C7
Givat Hayim (Me'uhad)
15 C7
Giv'at Hemda 52 G20
Giv'at Hen 15 C9
Giv'at Hevya 5 E4
Giv'ati 27 C12
Giv'ati Memorial ....
27 B11
Giv'at Iv'ha 41 C17
Giv'at Keder 4 C18
Giv'at Kevuda . 4 C-D17
Giv'at Ko'ah 22 D9
Giv'at Laham 6 E4
Giv'at Mesura ....
42 D16-17
Giv'at Moran 34 D13
Givat Nili 11 C6
Giv'at Noah (Ju'ara) .....
12 D6
Giv'at Oz 12 D6
Giv'at Pu'a 58 F24
Giv'at Refed 39 E16
Giv'at Rut 4 C17
Giv'at Sasgon 58 G23
Giv'at Sha'at 2 G14
Giv'at Shapira ... 15 C9
Giv'at Shemen .. 42 D15
Giv'at Shemesh (Instit.)
25 D11
Giv'at Shfifon ... 37 F15
Giv'at Shmu'el .. 22 C9
Giv'at Tzafit 37 F15
Giv'at Ye'arim .. 20 E11
Giv'at Yeshayahu ....
25 D12
Giv'at Yo'av 4 F4
Giv'at Ze'ev 20 E10
Giv'olim 33 B-C14
Giv'on Hahadasha ....
20 E10
Giv'ot Bar 33 C14
Giv'ot Goral 34 D14
Giv'ot Kadma'i .. 37 F15
Giv'ot Lahav 34 D14
Giv'ot Loven 52 G20
Giv'ot Shehoret 58 G24
Giv'ot Sheizaf .. 46 G17
Giv'ot Tlimon 11 C6
Giv'ot Tzehiha .. 52 F21
Giv'ot Tziya 54 E19
Givton 21 C11
Gizo 19 D11
Globusland 20 E11
Golan 2 F-G2
Golan Field School 2 F3
Gonen 1 F2
Goren 8 D3
Granot Hagalil .. 8 D3
Grofit 56 G22
Gulf of Eilat 58 G25
Gush Halav ancient
synagogue 5 E3
Gush Segev 5 D4

Guz Abu Sheqafa ....
43 A16
Guz es Saham 43 A16
Gva'ot 26 E11
Gvar'am 27 B13
Gvat 12 D5
Gvulot 44 B15
H
Ha'arava (Arabah) ....
52 G20
Habla 15 D9
Habonim 11 C6
Hadar Am 15 C9
Hadasim 15 C9
Hadera 15 C7
Hadera Ma'arav Station
15 C7
Hadid 22 D10
Had Nes 3 F3
Ha'emek Hane'elam ......
9 E6
Hafetz Hayim 28 C11
Hagai 23 E13
Hagesher Haturki ....
33 C14
Hagor 22 C9
Hagoshrim 20 F1
Hahagana Station (Tel
Aviv) 21 C10
Hahof Hashaket
(Kinneret) 3 F4
Hahotrim 11 C5
Hai Bar 11 C5
Haifa 11 C5
Haifa Airport 11 C5
Haifa Port 11 C5
Haifa University . 11 C5
Hajajra 12 D5
Hajeh 16 D8
Hakastel 20 E11
Hakfar Hayarok . 21 C9
Halaf 12 D5
Halamish (Neveh Tzuf)
19 E9
Halashon (Tongue) ......
2 G13
Halhul 23 E12
Halutz 8 D3
Hama'apil 15 C7
Hamachtesh Hagadol ...
39 E16
Hamachtesh Hakatan ...
37 F16
Hamadiya 10 F6
Hamam 6 E4
Hamam el Malih (Hot
Springs) 14 F7
Hamapal Halavan 4 G4
Hamapal Hashahor ......
4 G4
Hamat Gader (El
Hama) 3 F5
Hamei Mazor 2 G13
Hamei Shalem ... 24 G12
Hameishar 51 F19
Hamei Yishai ... 24 G13
Hamei Zohar 2 G14
Hamra 14 F8
Hanakik Hashahor 3 F3
Hanaton 5 D5
Hani'el 15 C9
Hanita 7 C3
Hanot Tagarim ... 9 E5
Ha'ogen 15 C7
Ha'on 3 F4
Hapitriya 58 F23

Har Adami 6 E5
Har Adar 20 E11
Har Adir 8 D3
Har Admon 1 E3
Har Afor 48 E18
Har Ahino'am 10 E6
Har Akev 47 E17
Har Akrav 47 D18
Har Alon 2 F1
Har Amasa 31 E14
Har Amir 58 G24
Har Arbel 6 E4
Har Ardon 48 E18
Har Argaman 56 G23
Har Aricha 47 D18
Har Arif 54 E20
Hararit 5 E4
Har Arkov 47 D17
Har Asa 58 F25
Harashim 8 D3
Har Atzmon 5 D4
Har Avinadav 9 E6
Har Avishai 24 F13
Har Avital 2 G2
Har Avivim 1 E2
Har Avnon 39 E16
Har Avtalyon 5 E4
Har Ayarim 4 C19
Har Ayelet 1 E3
Har Ayit 56 G22
Har Badar 29 F13
Har Badod 38 G15
Har Bani Rasan 2 G2
Har Barir 29 F14
Har Barkan 9 E6
Har Bar'on 2 F2
Har Bar Yohai 5 E3
Har Batur 53 D20
Har Bek'a 39 D15
Har Bental 2 G2
Har Ben Ya'ir 2 F13
Har Berech 58 F23
Har Bezek 13 E7
Har Biranit 8 D3
Har Bosmat 57 F23
Har Dalton 6 E3
Har Darga 46 F18
Har Daya 37 F15
Har Dla'at 54 D20
Har Dov 2 F1
Har Dovev 5 E3
Harduf 8 D5
Har Dvora 9 E5
Harei Anim 31 E14
Harei Dimona 39 E15
Harei Ef'eh 37 F15
Harei Gilbo'a 9 E6
Harei Hachlil 58 G23
Harei Hatira 39 E16
Harei Ira 31 E14
Harei Meiron 5 E3
Harei Natzeret 9 E5
Harei Shezor 5 D4
Har Eival (Mt. Ebal) ....
  13 E8
Harei Yatir 31 E14
Harei Yodfat 5 D4
Har'el 19 D11
Har Eldad 47 D17
Har Enmar 45 F18
Har Eshet 52 G20
Har Etzem 39 E15
Har Evyatar 6 E3
Har Ezuz 4 C18

Har Gadir 14 F7
Har Gamal 8 D4
Har Gavnunim ... 29 F14
Har Gavri'el 54 D20
Har Gazam 45 F19
Har Gevim 46 F18
Har Giborim 9 E6
Har Gilo 23 E11
Har Gilo Field School ....
  23 E11
Har Gilon 5 D4
Har Godrim 5 E3
Har Golhan 37 F16
Har Grafon 48 E18
Har Grizim (Mt.
  Gerizim) 13 E8
Har Grofit 56 G22
Har Ha'ahim 5 E4
Har Ha'ari 5 E3
Har Habetarim 2 F1
Har Hacarmel (Mt.
  Carmel) 11 C5
Har Hadav 45 F19
Har Hadav 51 F19
Har Hakotz 5 E4
Har Halamish 54 E20
Har Halukim 39 D16
Har Halutz 8 D3
Har Hamarmar 38 G15
Har Hame'ara 53 D20
Har Hameishar . 51 F19
Har Hamenuhot 20 E11
Har Hamran 4 C18
Har Hanegev Field
  School 48 E18
Har Hardon 29 F13
Har Harduf 29 F13
Har Haribi 8 D5
Har Harif 53 D19
Har Haroz 54 E20
Har Haru'ah 20 E11
Har Hasha'avi 5 D4
Har Hatayasim .. 20 E11
Har Hatzera 37 F16
Har Hazon 5 E4
Har Hehalak 37 F17
Har Hemet 47 D18
Har Hermon 2 F1
Har Hermonit 2 G1
Har Heter 2 F14
Har Hetzron 29 F13
Har Hillel 5 E3
Har Hisun 54 D20
Har Hizkiyahu .. 57 F24
Har Hogen 55 F23
Har Holed 29 F13
Har Horsha 4 C19
Har Horshan 11 C6
Har Hozeh 5 E4
Haris 19 D9
Harish 16 D7
Har Itai 29 F13
Har Kabir 13 E8
Har Kadarim 5 E4
Har Kadim 29 F15
Har Kahal 2 F1
Har Kamun 5 E4
Har Kana'im 2 F14
Har Karkom 54 E20
Har Kaskasim 39 E16
Har Katum 48 E18
Har Kavul 8 D4
Har Kdumim 9 E5
Har Kefir 5 E3
Har Keren 41 C16

Har Ketura 56 G22
Har Kidod 29 F14
Har Kimrir 29 F15
Har Kipa 52 F19
Har Kirton 54 E19
Har Kna'an 6 E3
Har Komot 38 F15
Har Kotar 5 E3
Har Kramim 2 F1
Har Ksulot 9 E5
Har Lehavim 34 D14
Har Leta'ot 29 F14
Har Lotz 53 D19
Har Mahbir 51 F19
Har Malkishu'a ... 10 F6
Har Manor 8 D3
Har Marpek 48 E18
Har Marzeva 45 F17
Har Matat 8 D3
Har Mehalel 11 C5
Har Meidad 47 D17
Har Meiron 5 E3
Har Meiron Field
  School 5 E3
Har Menahem ... 29 F14
Har Menorim 3 F4
Har Menuha 52 F20
Har Micha'el 54 E20
Har Michrot 58 G23
Har Mihya 47 D17
Har Mirbatz 3 E15
Har Montar 18 F11
Har Na'atzutz ... 56 F22
Har Nafha 47 D18
Har Nahum 3 F4
Har Na'im 42 D15
Har Namer 29 F13
Har Nekarot 45 F18
Har Neriya 5 E3
Har Nes 53 D20
Har Nezer 1 E2
Har Nishpeh 52 F19
Har Nitai 6 E4
Har Nitzim 3 E15
Har Noked 39 D15
Har Oded 54 D19
Har Odem 2 F1
Har Omer 46 F18
Har Ora 58 G24
Har Parot 56 F22
Har Peki'in 8 D3
Har Peres 4 G3
Har Pitam 48 E19
Har Rabud 31 E13
Har Ram 2 F1
Har Ramon 53 D19
Har Ravid 6 E4
Har Ravitz 5 E3
Har Raviv 4 C17
Har Rechev 48 E17
Har Rehav'am ... 58 F25
Har Resisim 4 C18
Har Retamim 47 D17
Har Romem 53 D19
Har Rut 4 C17
Har Sa'ad 48 E18
Har Safun 4 C17
Har Sagi 53 D20
Har Sansan 26 E11
Har Sansana 34 D14
Har Saraf 37 F15
Har Sasa 5 E3
Har Sdom 38 G15
Har Seguv 57 F23

Har Sha'alav 56 G21
Har Shahar 39 D16
Har Shaharut 56 G22
Har Shahmon 58 G24
Har Shahrur 56 F22
Har Shaked 2 F1
Har Shalhavit 2 F1
Har Shalhevet 29 F14
Har Shani 57 F24
Har Sha'ul 9 E6
Har Shazar 54 E20
Har Shehoret 58 F24
Har Shezif 2 F1
Har Shezor 8 D3
Har Shifra 1 E3
Har Shipon 2 G2
Har Shizafon 56 G21
Har Shlomo 58 F25
Har Shokaf 11 C5
Har Sna'im 2 F1
Har Sumak 11 C5
Har Tamun 14 F8
Har Tavor (Mt. Tabor) .
  9 E5
Har Teref 48 E17
Har Timna 58 G23
Har Tir'an 5 E4
Har Tzavo'a 39 D16
Har Tzayad 3 E16
Har Tze'elim 29 F14
Har Tzefahot 58 G25
Har Tzefira 29 F14
Har Tzemed 3 E16
Har Tzenifim 55 F21
Har Tzeruya 24 G13
Har Tzin (Mt. Hor) ....
  37 F17
Har Tzuri'oz 54 E20
Harutzim 15 C9
Har Uziyahu 58 F24
Har Varda 2 F1
Har Ya'ala 25 D11
Har Ya'alon 56 G21
Har Yahav 45 F18
Har Yahel 29 F14
Har Yavne'el 10 F5
Har Yedidya 58 G24
Har Ye'elim 29 F14
Har Yeho'ahaz .. 58 F24
Har Yehoram 58 F24
Har Yehoshafat .. 58 F25
Har Yelek 48 E19
Har Yitzpor 10 E6
Har Yo'ash 58 F25
Har Yonatan 2 G14
Har Yosifon 2 G2
Har Zevul 8 D3
Har Zichrona 11 C6
Har Ziv 8 D3
Hashayara Memorial ....
  7 C3
Hashmona'im .. 19 D10
Hasolelim 12 D5
Haspin 4 G4
Hativat Hanegev
  Monument 34 D14
Hatrurim 29 F14
Hatzar Addar 29 F14
Hatzar Deganya .. 10 F5
Hatzar Kinneret .. 10 F5
Hatzav 28 C11
Hatzerim 33 C15
Hatzeva 46 G17
Hatzor Ashdod . 27 C11
Hatzor Haglilit 6 E3

Hatzrot Ha'ikarim 9 E5
Hatzrot Ko'ah 22 D9
Hatzrot Yasaf 7 C4
Havat Baba Yona .. 1 F3
Havat Bat Ya'ar .. 6 E3
Havat Ha'alpakot
(Alpaca Farm) .. 47 E18
Havat Hashomer ... 5 E5
Havat Karmei Avdat ......
47 D17
Havatzelet Hasharon .....
15 C9
Hayarmuk 10 F5
Hayogev 12 D6
Hazon 5 E4
Hazore'a 12 D6
Hazor'im 3 F5
Hebrew University
(Jerusalem) 20 E11
Hebron (Hevron) ....
23 E12
Hebron Bypass .. 23 E12
Heftzi Ba 10 E6
Heletz 27 C13
Hemdat 14 F8
Hemdat Yamim 5 E3
Hemed 22 C10
Henyon Nahal Sarach ..
8 D3
Herev Le'et 15 C7
Hermesh 16 D7
Hermon Field School ..
1 F1
Herut 15 C9
Herzliya 15 C9
Herzliya Pitu'ah .. 15 C9
Herzliya Station .. 21 C9
Hevel Shalom 43 A15
Hever 9 E6
Hibat Tziyon 15 C7
Hila 8 D3
Hinanit 12 D6
Hisham's Palace
(Khirbet el Mafjar) .....
18 F10
Hizma 17 F10
Hod Hasharon 22 C9
Hodiya 27 B12
Hodiyot (Educ. cntr.) ..
6 E4
Hof Accadia 21 C9
Hof Afridar 27 B12
Hof Almog 58 G25
Hof Amnon 3 F3
Hof Amud 3 F4
Hof Arbel 3 F4
Hof Barne'a 27 B12
Hof Bat Galim 7 C4
Hof Benyamin .. 18 G11
Hof Berenike 3 F4
Hof Dado 11 C5
Hof Dekel 3 F4
Hof Duga 3 F4
Hof Dugit 3 F4
Hof Ein Bokek 2 G14
Hof Ein Gedi 24 G12
Hof Gai 3 F4
Hof Giv'at Aliya 21 B10
Hof Gofra 3 F4
Hof Golan (Luna Gal) ..
3 F4
Hof Hacarmel 11 C5
Hof Hacarmel Field
School 11 C6
Hof Hadolphinim ....
58 G25

Hof Ha'ela 3 F4
Hof Halukim 3 F4
Hof Hariviera ... 21 B10
Hof Hasela 21 B10
Hof Hashaket 7 C4
Hof Hasharon 15 C9
Hof Hatzuk 21 C9
Hof Hawaii 3 F4
Hof Ilanot 3 F4
Hofit 15 C7
Hof Kahal 3 F5
Hof Kalya (Water Park)
18 G10
Hof Kaneh 3 F4
Hof Kinar 3 F4
Hof Kursi 3 F4
Hof Levanon 3 F4
Hof Magdala (Christian
holy site) 3 F4
Hof Marina 21 B10
Hof Mineral 24 G12
Hof Nitzanim 27 B12
Hof Palmahim .. 21 B10
Hof Rotem 3 F4
Hof Sapirit 3 F4
Hof Shahaf 3 F4
Hof Shaldag 3 F5
Hof Sheizaf 3 F4
Hof Sheraton 21 C9
Hof Shikmim 3 F4
Hof Shitim 3 F4
Hof Siesta 18 G11
Hof Sironit 3 F4
Hof Susita 3 F4
Hof Tamar 3 F4
Hof Tel Baruch .. 21 C9
Hof Tze'elon 3 F4
Hof Tzemah 3 F5
Hof Tziltzal 3 F4
Hof Tzinabrei 3 F4
Hof Yerushalayim ..
21 C9
Hof Zamir 11 C5
Hof Zikim 27 B13
Hogla 15 C7
Holit 43 A15
Holon 21 C10
Holot Agur (Agur
Sands) 44 B16
Holot Ashdod ....
27 B11-12
Holot Ashkelon . 27 B12
Holot Halutza (Halutza
Sands) 44 B-C16
Holot Rishon Letziyon ..
21 B10
Holot Shunra 41 C16
Holot Yavneh 21 B11
Horashim 15 D9
Horbat Adulam 25 D12
Horbat Amudim 5 E4
Horbat Aristobuliya ..
32 E13
Horbat Aro'er ... 39 E15
Horbat Be'er Resisim ..
50 C18
Horbat Breicha 33 C13
Horbat Buch 39 E15
Horbat Butzin 12 D5
Horbat Dafit 58 G24
Horbat Dragot .. 31 E14
Horbat Ein Gedi 24 G12
Horbat Eshtemo'a ....
31 E13
Horbat Giv'it 17 F9

Horbat Gov Yosef .. 6 E3
Horbat Halukim ....
39 D17
Horbat Haro'eh 39 E16
Horbat Hartuv .. 25 D11
Horbat Hatzatza ....
39 D17
Horbat Hipushit ....
41 C15
Horbat Karkor Ilit ....
34 D14
Horbat Kasif 31 E14
Horbat Katzra .. 46 F18
Horbat Keshet 12 D5
Horbat Kobi 23 E11
Horbat Mamshit
(Kurnub) 37 F16
Horbat Ma'on Banegev
35 B14
Horbat Midras .. 25 D12
Horbat Minim 3 F4
Horbat Mizbah . 31 E15
Horbat Nitzana . 49 B17
Horbat Paku'a ... 42 D16
Horbat Patish ... 33 C14
Horbat Rahba ... 39 E15
Horbat Rehovot
Banegev 41 C16
Horbat Rogem ... 41 C16
Horbat Rosh Zayit 8 D4
Horbat Sa'adim . 23 E11
Horbat Sa'adon 41 C16
Horbat Sansana 34 D14
Horbat Shema 5 E3
Horbat Sindina ... 2 G2
Horbat Snunit 3 F3
Horbat Sokho ... 25 D12
Horbat Susya ... 31 E13
Horbat Tefen 8 D4
Horbat Timna 58 F23
Horbat Tzafir 37 F16
Horbat Yatir 31 E14
Horbat Yavneh Yam .....
21 B10
Horbat Zif 23 E13
Horbat Zro'a 12 D5
Horvot Atlit 11 C5
Horvot Caesarea . 11 C7
Horvot Halutza 41 C15
Horvot Qumran ....
18 G11
Horvot Yodfat 5 D4
Hosen 8 D3
Hoshaya 12 D5
Hotzeh Shomron 19 D9
Hukok 6 E4
Hula 1 E2
Hulata 1 F2-3
Hula Valley 1 F2
Hulda 22 C11
Hulikat Memorial
Gedud 53 .... 27 C12
Hura 34 D14
Hurfeish 8 D3
Hurkanya (Khirbet el
Mird) 18 F11
Husan 23 E11
Huwara 13 E8

I
I'bilin 8 D4
Ibthan 16 D7
Ibtin 12 C5
Ichilov Hos. 21 C9
Idan 38 G17
Idna 25 D12

Ijnisinya 13 E8
Iksal 9 E5
Iktaba 16 D8
Ilaniya (Sejera) 5 E5
Ilanot 15 C9
I'lar 16 D7
Ilut 12 D5
Imanu'el 16 D8
Imatin 16 D8
Industrial Area Bar On
13 E8
Industrial Area Brosh
(Ma'arav) 25 D11
Intisar (Buqei'a el
Gharbiya) 8 D3
Iraq Burin 13 E8
Ir Ovot 38 G17
Irtah 16 D8
Isfiya 11 C5
Iskaka 13 E9
Itamar 13 E8

J
Jaba (Samaria) 13 E7
Jaba (near Ramallah) ....
20 E10
Jabaliyeh 36 B13
Jabaliyeh (Refugee
Camp) 36 B13
Jaffa Port 21 C9
Jalameh 9 E6
Jalazun 20 E10
Jalbun 10 E6
Jaljulya 22 C9
Jalqamus 9 E7
Jalud 20 E9
Jama'in 13 E9
Jamala 19 D10
Jamliya 4 G4
Janiyeh 20 E10
Jarba 13 E7
Jat (Samaria) 16 D7
Jat (Galilee) 8 D3
Jayus 16 D8
Jebel Batin Halaweh ....
20 E9
Jebel el Hufeira 46 G18
Jebel Harmun 18
G10-11
Jebel Hureish 13 E7
Jenin 9 E6
Jericho (Yeriho) ....
18 F-G10
Jericho Bypass .. 18 G10
Jericho Synagogue ....
18 F10
Jerusalem 20 E11
Jerusalem 23 E11
Jezreel Valley 9 E6
Jibya 20 E10
Jifna (Gophna) .. 20 E10
Jiljiliyeh 20 E9
Jinsafut 16 D8
Jish (Gush Halav) .. 5 E3
Jisr ez Zarqa 11 C6
Jit 13 E8
Jordan Park 3 F3
Jordan Park Reserve ...
3 F3
Jordan River 3 F3
Jordan River Terminal
10 F6
Judaica Center . 23 E12
Judea 23 E-F11-12
Judean Desert .. 24 F11
Judeida-Makr 7 C4

Judeideh 13 E7
Judeira 20 E10
Julis 8 D4
Juneid 13 E8
Jurdeih 8 D3
Jureish 13 E9

K

Ka'abiya 12 D5
Kabri 7 C3
Kabul (Kavul) 8 D4
Kadarim 6 E4
Kadesh Barne'a 49 C18
Kadima 15 C9
Kadita 5 E3
Kadoorie (Regional
Cnt.) 9 E5
Kadoorie School 9 E5
Kafr Abush 16 D8
Kafr Aqab 20 E10
Kafr Bara 22 D9
Kafr ed Dik 19 D9
Kafr Ein 19 D9
Kafr el Labad 16 D8
Kafr Jamal 16 D8
Kafr Kama 9 E5
Kafr Kana 5 E5
Kafr Kila 1 E1
Kafr Kud 12 D7
Kafr Laqif 16 D8
Kafr Malik 20 E-F9
Kafr Manda 5 D4
Kafr Misr 9 E5
Kafr Ni'meh 19 D10
Kafr Qadum 16 D8
Kafr Qalil 13 E8
Kafr Qari' 12 C-D6
Kafr Qasim 22 D9
Kafr Ra'i 16 D7
Kafr Ruman 16 D8
Kafr Sumei' 8 D3
Kafr Sur 16 D8
Kafr Thulth 16 D9
Kafr Yasif 7 D4
Kafr Zibad 16 D8
Kahal 6 E4
Kalanit 6 E4
Kalya 18 G11
Kamana 5 E4
Kamun 5 E4
Kanaf 3 F3
Kanot 28 C11
Kanyon Shehoret ......
58 G24
Karawet Bani Hasan ......
16 D9
Karei Desheh 3 F4
Karkom 3 F3
Karmei Tzur .. 23 E12
Karmei Yosef 22 D11
Karmel 29 F13
Karmi'el 5 D4
Karmil 32 E13
Karmiya 27 B13
Karnei Hitin 6 E4
Karnei Ramon .. 47 D19
Karnei Shomron 16 D8
Karzeh 31 E13
Katzir-Harish 12 D7
Katzrin 2 F3
Kaukab Abu el Hija ......
5 D4
Kawbar 20 E10
Kayakei Kfar Blum ......
20 F2

Kedma (Youth Village)
28 C12
Kedumim 16 D8
Kedumim Ilit 16 D8
Keidar (temporary) ......
17 F11
Keidar 17 F11
Kel'a 2 F2
Kelil 8 D3
Kemehin 49 B17
Kenyon Nahal Sad ......
33 C13
Kerem Ben Shemen ......
22 D10
Kerem Ben Zimra .. 1 E3
Kerem Maharal .. 11 C6
Kerem Shalom .. 43 A15
Kerem Shalom Crossing
43 A15
Keren Carmel
(Muhraka) 12 D5
Keren Naftali 1 E2
Keren Sartaba
(Alexandrion) 14 F9
Kesalon 19 D11
Keshet 2 G3
Keshet Yonatan Field
School 2 G3
Ketef Hermon 2 F1
Ketef Hetzron 29 F13
Ketef Si'on 2 F1
Ketef Tur 24 F12
Ketura 56 G22
Ketzi'ot 49 C17
Kever Rabbi Akiva 3 F4
Kever Rabbi Halafta ......
5 E4
Kever Rabbi Meir Ba'al
Hanes 3 F4
Kever Rabbi Oshaya
Demin Tirya 8 D3
Kever Rabbi Shim'on ....
5 E3
Kever Rahel 23 E11
Kever Yosef 13 E8
Kfar Adumim 17 F10
Kfar Ahim 28 C11
Kfar Aviv 27 C11
Kfar Avoda 15 C9
Kfar Aza 36 B13
Kfar Azar 21 C9
Kfar Baram ancient
synagogue 5 E3
Kfar Baruch 12 D5
Kfar Bialik 7 C4
Kfar Bilu 22 C11
Kfar Bin Nun 19 D11
Kfar Blum 1 E2
Kfar Dani'el 22 D10
Kfar Eldad 23 F11
Kfar Etzyon 23 E12
Kfar Etzyon Field
School 23 E12
Kfar Galim 11 C5
Kfar Gid'on 9 E5
Kfar Giladi 1 E1
Kfar Glickson 11 C7
Kfar Habad 22 C10
Kfar Habad Station ......
22 C10
Kfar Habaptistim 22 C9
Kfar Hahoresh .. 12 D5
Kfar Hamaccabi .. 12 C5
Kfar Hanagid .. 21 C11
Kfar Hananya 5 E4
Kfar Hanasi 3 F3

Kfar Hano'ar Hadati .....
12 C5
Kfar Hano'ar Nitzanim
27 B12
Kfar Hanofesh Achziv ..
7 C3
Kfar Hanokdim .. 29 F14
Kfar Ha'oranim 19 D10
Kfar Harif 28 C11
Kfar Haro'eh 15 C7
Kfar Haruv 3 F4
Kfar Hashmonai ......
19 D10
Kfar Hasidim A 11 C5
Kfar Hasidim B 11 C5
Kfar Havradim 8 D3
Kfar Hayim 15 C9
Kfar Hess 15 C9
Kfar Hitim 6 E4
Kfar Hoshen (Sifsufa) ..
5 E3
Kfar Kisch 9 E5
Kfar Maimon .. 36 B14
Kfar Malal 15 C9
Kfar Masaryk 7 C4
Kfar Menahem . 28 C11
Kfar Monash 15 C9
Kfar Mordechai 28 C11
Kfar Netter 15 C9
Kfar Pines 11 C7
Kfar Rosh Hanikra 7 C3
Kfar Ruppin 10 F6
Kfar Rut 19 D10
Kfar Saba 15 C9
Kfar Shamai 5 E3
Kfar Shmaryahu . 15 C9
Kfar Shmu'el ... 22 D10
Kfar Shumi (Shuni) ......
11 C6
Kfar Silver 27 B12
Kfar Syrkin 22 C9
Kfar Szold 1 F2
Kfar Tapu'ah 13 E9
Kfar Tavor (Mes'ha) ....
9 E5
Kfar Truman 22 D10
Kfar Uriya 25 D11
Kfar Vitkin 15 C7
Kfar Vradim 8 D3
Kfar Warburg .. 27 C12
Kfar Ya'betz 15 C9
Kfar Yehezkel 9 E6
Kfar Yehoshua .. 12 D5
Kfar Yona 15 C9
Kfar Zeitim 6 E4
Khalet el Fuleh .. 14 F8
Khan 19 D11
Khan el Hatruri (Inn of
the Good Samaritan) ..
17 F10
Khan Hashayarot ......
47 D17
Khan Yunis .. 35 A14
Kharas 25 E12
Kharaseh 31 E13
Kharbata 19 D10
Khashm el Karem ......
29 F13
Khawalid 8 D5
Khirbet Abdallah
Ibrahim 23 E11
Khirbet Abu Falah ......
20 E9
Khirbet Asala 16 D9
Khirbet Beit Anun ......
23 E12

Khirbet Beit Hasan ......
14 F8
Khirbet Birket el Qasr ..
17 F9
Khirbet ed Deir .. 23 F12
Khirbet el Adas 43 A15
Khirbet el Arba'in ......
10 F6
Khirbet el Ashqar ......
16 D9
Khirbet el Awja et
Tahta 18 F9
Khirbet el Burj 20 E9
Khirbet El Humeidiyeh
23 E11
Khirbet el Karmil
(Carmel) 32 E13
Khirbet el
Manqushiyeh 24 F12
Khirbet El Misbah ......
19 D10
Khirbet el Mudawar ......
16 D9
Khirbet el Mutileh ......
10 E7
Khirbet en Nabi Elyas ..
16 D8
Khirbet es Sumayeh ......
25 D13
Khirbet et Tayibeh ......
12 D6
Khirbet Ikhza'a 35 A15
Khirbet Jub er Rum ......
17 F11
Khirbet Kanaf 3 F3
Khirbet Karmeh 31 E13
Khirbet Ma'in (Maon) .
32 E13
Khirbet Marjameh ......
17 F9
Khirbet Mo'a 46 G18
Khirbet Qeila (Keilah) ..
25 D12
Khirbet Qeis 20 E9
Khirbet Ramantaniya ..
2 G3
Khirbet Ras Atiya ......
16 D9
Khirbet Sahba .. 23 F12
Khirbet Shuna .. 10 F5
Khirbet Shuweikeh
31 E13
Khirbet Sir 16 D8
Khirbet Somaq .. 11 C5
Khirbet Tuqu'a .. 23 E12
Khirbet Tura 12 D7
Khirbet Yanun .. 14 F8
Kidmat Tzvi 2 F3
Kidron 28 C11
Kifl Harith 13 E9
King Husein Bridge
(Allenby) Border
Crossing 18 G10
Kinneret (Kvutza) ......
10 F5
Kinneret (Moshava) ......
3 F5
Kipat Eshet .. 52 G20
Kipat Hemda .. 52 F20
Kipat Paran .. 52 F20
Kipros (Cyprus) 18 F10
Kiryat Anavim .. 20 E11
Kiryat Arba .. 23 E12
Kiryat Ata 11 C5
Kiryat Bialik 7 C4
Kiryat Ekron 22 C11
Kiryat Gat 28 C12

Kiryat Hadassah 20 E11
Kiryat Hatechni'on
11 C5
Kiryat Malachi . 28 C12
Kiryat Motzkin 7 C4
Kiryat Motzkin Station
7 C4
Kiryat Netafim 16 D9
Kiryat Ono 22 C9
Kiryat Shmona 1 E2
Kiryat Tiv'on 12 D5
Kiryat Yam 7 C4
Kiryat Ye'arim 20 E11
Kishon Port 11 C5
Kishor 8 D4
Kisra-Sumei' 8 D3
Kisufim 35 B14
Klahim 33 C13
Kochav Hashahar 17 F9
Kochav Michael Sobell
27 C12
Kochav Ya'akov (Abir
Ya'akov) 20 E10
Kochav Ya'ir 16 D8
Komemiyut 28 C12
Koranit 5 D4
Korazim 3 F3
Kramim 34 D14
Kseifa 32 E14
Kufeir 13 E7
Kufeirat 12 D7
Kur 16 D8
Kuwaiya 4 G4
Kvish Allon 14 F7-8
Kvish Haminharot
23 E11
Kvish Hatzafon 8 D3
Kvish Hotzeh Shomron
13 E9
Kvish Hotzeh Yisra'el
11 C6
Kvish Wadi Ara . 12 D6
Kvish Wadi Milek
11 C6
Kvutzat Yavneh 27 C11

L
Labuna 7 C3
Lachish 25 D12
Ladder of Tyre 7 C3
Lahav 34 D14
Lahavot Habashan
20 F2
Lahavot Haviva 15 C7
Lake Kinneret 3 F4
Lapid 19 D10
Lapidot 8 D3
Laqiya 34 D14
Latrun armoured cars .
19 D11
Latrun Monastery
19 D11
Lavi 6 E4
Lavon 5 D4
Lehavim 34 D14
Lev Yatir 31 E14
Liman 7 C3
Little Switzerland
11 C5
Livnim 6 E4
Lod 22 C10
Lod Station 22 C10
Lohamei Hageta'ot
7 C4
Lotan 56 G22
Lotem 5 E4

Lower Beit Horon - see
Beit Horon et Tahta
Luban Sharqiyeh 20 E9
Luzit 25 D12

M
Ma'abarot 15 C7
Ma'agalim 33 C14
Ma'agan 3 F5
Ma'agan Micha'el
11 C6
Ma'agar Bazelet 4 G3
Ma'agar Beit Netofa
5 D5
Ma'agar Bental 2 F2
Ma'agar Bnei Yisra'el
4 G3
Ma'agar Daliyot 4 G3
Ma'agar Dalton 5 E3
Ma'agar Hital 4 G4
Ma'agar Keshet 4 G3
Ma'agar Kfar Baruch
12 D5
Ma'agar Ramantaniya .
2 G2
Ma'agar Revaya 4 G3
Ma'agar Shikma
(Seasonal) 27 B13
Ma'agar Tirtza 14 G9
Ma'agar Tzalmon . 5 E4
Ma'agar Yekutza . 4 G4
Ma'agar Yeroham
39 E16
Ma'agar Yosifon 2 G2
Ma'agar Zohar . 27 C12
Ma'agurot Dimona
39 E15
Ma'agurot Etzem
39 E15
Ma'agurot Kedem
4 C18
Ma'agurot Sa'adon
41 C16
Ma'aleh Adumim
17 F11
Ma'aleh Afor 48 E18
Ma'aleh Akrabim
37 F16
Ma'aleh Amos 23 F12
Ma'aleh Arod 53 D19
Ma'aleh Beit Horon
20 E10
Ma'aleh Ben Ya'ir
2 G13
Ma'aleh Dragot 31 E14
Ma'aleh Efra'im 14 F9
Ma'aleh Eilat . 58 F-G25
Ma'aleh Eli 37 F16
Ma'aleh Gamla 3 F3
Ma'aleh Gilboa 10 E6
Ma'aleh Ha'atzma'ut
48 E18
Ma'aleh Hahamisha
20 E11
Ma'aleh Hameishar
51 F19
Ma'aleh Hatzera
37 F16
Ma'aleh Isi'im 24 F-G13
Ma'aleh Levona . 20 E9
Ma'aleh Mahmal
48 E18
Ma'aleh Michmas
17 F10
Ma'aleh Mishmar
29 F13
Ma'aleh Namer . 29 F13
Ma'aleh Nurit 9 E6

Ma'aleh Paran 51 F20
Ma'aleh Ramon 47 E19
Ma'aleh Sagi . 54 D-E20
Ma'aleh Shai 14 F7
Ma'aleh Shomron
16 D8
Ma'aleh Tamar 38 G15
Ma'alot Tarshiha . 8 D3
Ma'anit 15 C7
Ma'arav Galil-Achziv
Field School 7 C3
Ma'as 22 C9
Ma'avar Erez (Erez
Crossing) 36 B13
Ma'avar Karni . 36 B13
Ma'avar Katif . 35 A14
Ma'avar Nahal Oz
36 B13
Ma'ayan Baruch . 1 E1
Ma'ayan Tzvi 11 C6
Mabu'im 33 C13
Maccabim 19 D10
Machtesh Hatira
39 E16
Machtesh Hatzera
37 F16
Machtesh Ramon
48 E18
Madama 13 E8
Magal 16 D7
Magen 36 B15
Magen Sha'ul 9 E6
Maghar 5 E4
Magshimim 22 C9
Mahana'im 3 F3
Mahana'im Airport
3 F3
Mahaneh Hama'pilim .
11 C5
Mahaneh Yatir . 31 E14
Mahseya 25 D11
Maintenance Corps
Memorial 22 D10
Majdal Bani Fadil 14 F9
Majdal Islim 1 E2
Majdal Shams 2 F1
Majd el Krum 8 D4
Malha Station
(Jerusalem) 26 E11
Malka 4 G5
Malkishu'a 10 E6
Malkiya 1 E2
Manof 5 D4
Manot 7 D3
Manshiyet Zabda
12 D5
Ma'of 29 F14
Ma'on 29 F13
Ma'or 15 C7
Ma'oz Hayim 10 F6
Ma'oz Tziyon 20 E11
Mapal Ayit 4 G3
Mapal Banias 2 F1
Mapal Dvora 2 F2
Mapalei Daliyot 4 G3
Mapalei Gamla 4 G3
Mapalei Nahal Iyon
1 E1
Mapal Gilbon 2 F3
Mapal Sa'ar 2 F1
Mapal Zavitan 3 F3
Maqam er Ra'i 18 F10
Maqura 11 C6
Marda 13 E9
Margaliyot 1 E2
Marj Ayun 1 E1

Marj en-Na'ja 14 F8
Markabe 1 E1
Mar Saba Monastery
24 F11
Marun er Ras 1 E2
Masad 5 E4
Masada (Metzada)
2 G13
Masada 10 F5
Mas'ada 2 F1
Mas'ha 19 D9
Mash'abei Sadeh
42 D16
Mashen 27 B12
Mashhad 9 E5
Mashru' Musa Alami
18 G10
Maskiyot 14 F7
Maslul 33 C14
Masraq en Naj . 24 F11
Masu'a 14 F8
Masu'ot Yitzhak
27 C12
Mata 25 E11
Matan 15 D9
Matat 8 D3
Matityahu 19 D10
Matzli'ah 22 C10
Matzuva 7 C3
Mavki'im 27 B12
Mazari'en Nubani
20 E9
Mazkeret Batya 22 C11
Mazor 22 C9
Mazra'a 7 C3
Me'arat Adulam
25 D12
Me'arat Alma 1 E3
Me'arat Amira 6 E4
Me'arat Arubotayim
2 G15
Me'arat El Mishmash
23 E12
Me'arat Etzba 11 C5
Me'arat Habreicha
24 G12
Me'arat Ha'eima (Cave
of Horrors) 2 F13
Me'arat Ha'igrot (Cave
of Letters) 2 F-G13
Me'arat Hakemah
(Flour Cave) 38 G15
Me'arat Hamachpela
(Cave of the
Patriarchs) 23 E12
Me'arat Hamatmon
(Cave of Treasure)
2 F13
Me'arat Hanetifim
25 D11
Me'arat Haritun 23 F12
Me'arat Hate'omim
25 D11
Me'arat Kabara 11 C6
Me'arat Masu'a 25 D12
Me'arat Muraba'at
24 F12
Me'arat Pe'er 5 E3
Me'arat Sdom (Sodom
Cave) 38 G15
Me'arat Sechvi 6 E3
Me'arat Sorek 25 D11
Me'arat Wadi Salim
23 E11
Me'arat Yonim 8 D4
Me'arot Aviv 1 E2

Me'arot Beit Guvrin 25 D12
Me'arot Carmel 11 C6
Me'arot Hazan 25 D13
Me'arot Hever (Hever Caves) 2 F-G13
Me'arot Luzit 25 D12
Mechora 14 F8
Mefalsim 36 B13
Megadim 11 C5
Megiddo 12 D6
Megiddo Landing Strip 12 D6
Megiddo Prison 12 D6
Megilat Ha'esh Monument 25 E11
Mehlaf Ad Halom 27 B11
Mehlaf Adumim 17 F11
Mehlaf Aluf Sadeh 21 C9
Mehlaf Anava 22 D10
Mehlaf Ashdod 27 C11
Mehlaf Atlit 11 C5
Mehlaf Baqa-Jat 15 C7
Mehlaf Bar Ilan 21 C9
Mehlaf Bar Ilan Mizrah 21 C9
Mehlaf Ben Gurion 22 C10
Mehlaf Ben Shemen 22 D10
Mehlaf Caesarea 15 C7
Mehlaf Dani'el 22 D10
Mehlaf Dov Hos 21 C10
Mehlaf Ein Hakoreh 21 C10
Mehlaf Ein Tut 11 C6
Mehlaf Elifelet 6 E3
Mehlaf Elishama 15 C9
Mehlaf Elyakim 11 C6
Mehlaf Eyal 15 C9
Mehlaf Ganot 21 C10
Mehlaf Gan Raveh 21 C10
Mehlaf Gan Vradim 21 C10
Mehlaf Geha 21 C9
Mehlaf Gelilot 21 C9
Mehlaf Gelilot Mizrah 21 C9
Mehlaf Gil'am 7 D4
Mehlaf Giv'at Ko'ah 22 D9
Mehlaf Golda 20 E11
Mehlaf Hadarim 15 C9
Mehlaf Hagoshrim 1 F1
Mehlaf Hahalaha 21 C9
Mehlaf Haifa Darom 11 C5
Mehlaf Hakfar Hayarok 21 C9
Mehlaf Hakrayot (Checkpost) 11 C5
Mehlaf Harakevet 21 C9
Mehlaf Hashalom 21 C9
Mehlaf Hasira 21 C9
Mehlaf Havatzelet 15 C9
Mehlaf Herzliya 21 C9
Mehlaf Hof Hasharon 15 C9
Mehlaf Holon 21 C10

Mehlaf Holon Mizrah 21 C10
Mehlaf Holot 21 C10
Mehlaf Horashim 15 C9
Mehlaf Iksal 9 E5
Mehlaf Iron 12 C7
Mehlaf Keren Kayemet 21 C9
Mehlaf Kesem 22 C9
Mehlaf Kibbutz Galuyot 21 C10
Mehlaf Kiryat Rishon 21 C10
Mehlaf Komemiyut 21 C10
Mehlaf La Gardia 21 C9
Mehlaf Lahav 34 D14
Mehlaf Latrun 19 D11
Mehlaf Lod 22 C10
Mehlaf Ma'ahaz 33 C13
Mehlaf Matzli'ah 22 C10
Mehlaf Mesubim 21 C10
Mehlaf Mevo Ayalon 21 C10
Mehlaf Morasha 21 C9
Mehlaf Moshe Dayan 21 C10
Mehlaf Motza 20 E11
Mehlaf Nahshonim 22 C9
Mehlaf Nesharim 22 C10
Mehlaf Netanya 15 C9
Mehlaf Nitzanei Oz 16 D8
Mehlaf Olga 15 C7
Mehlaf Poleg 15 C9
Mehlaf Ra'anana 15 C9
Mehlaf Ra'anana Darom 22 C9
Mehlaf Ramla Darom 22 C10
Mehlaf Ramlod 22 C10
Mehlaf Rishon Darom 21 C10
Mehlaf Rishon Letziyon 21 C10
Mehlaf Rokah 21 C9
Mehlaf Rosh Ha'ayin 22 C9
Mehlaf Sha'ar Hagai 19 D11
Mehlaf Shapirim 22 C10
Mehlaf Shmaryahu 15 C9
Mehlaf Shmu'el 21 C9
Mehlaf Shoresh 19 E11
Mehlaf Sorek 28 C11
Mehlaf Tikva 22 C9
Mehlaf Wolffsohn 21 C10
Mehlaf Yadin 20 E11
Mehlaf Yanai 15 C7
Mehlaf Yarkon 22 C9
Mehlaf Yavneh 21 C11
Mehlaf Yoseftal 21 C10
Mehlaf Zarzir 12 D5
Mehlaf Zichron Ya'akov 11 C6
Mehola 14 F7
Mei Ami 12 D6

Mei Nefto'ah 20 E11
Meirav 10 F6
Meiron ancient synagogue 5 E3
Meir Shfeiya 11 C6
Meisar 15 D7
Meis el Jebel 1 E2
Meishar 27 C11
Meitar 34 D14
Meitav 9 E6
Meithalun 13 E7
Meitzar 4 G4
Melchet Villa 3 F4
Melei'a 12 D6
Meleihat Evrona 58 G24
Meleihat Yotvata 56 G23
Melilot 33 C14
Memorial to Sayeret Shaked 33 C14
Menahemya 10 F5
Menara 1 E2
Menuha 28 C12
Me'ona 8 D3
Merhav Am 39 D17
Merhavya (Kibbutz) 9 E6
Merhavya (Moshav) 9 E6
Merkaz Joe Alon 34 D14
Merkaz Shapira 27 C12
Merom Golan 2 F2
Mesilat Tziyon 19 D11
Mesilot 10 F6
Metulla 20 E1
Metzad Abirim 8 D3
Metzad Arugot 24 G13
Metzad Bokek 2 G14
Metzad Hatrurim 2 G14
Metzad Hatzeva 38 G17
Metzad Mahmal 48 E18
Metzad Mish'hor 48 E18
Metzad Nekarot 45 F18
Metzadot Yehuda 32 E13
Metzad Saharonim 48 E18
Metzad Shim'on 23 E12
Metzad Sorer 39 E15
Metzad Tamar 38 F15
Metzad Tzafir 37 F16
Metzad Yeroham 39 E16
Metzad Yorke'am 37 F16
Metzad Zohar 2 G14
Metzer 16 D7
Metzokei Arif 54 E19
Metzokei Lotz 53 D20
Metzudat Be'er Hafir 4 C18
Metzudat Gadin (Yehi'am) 8 D3
Metzudat Hunin 1 E2
Metzudat Patish 33 C14
Metzudat Yesha 1 E2
Metzudat Yo'av 27 C12
Metzukei Dragot 24 F12

Mevaseret Tziyon 20 E11
Mevo Beitar 26 E11
Mevo Dotan 16 D7
Mevo Hama 3 F4
Mevo Horon 19 D10
Mevo Modi'im 19 D10
Mheibib 1 E2
Michmanim 5 D4
Michmoret 15 C7
Midbar Paran (Paran Desert) 54 E21
Midbar Tzin (Zin Desert) 48 E17
Midrach Oz 12 D6
Midreshet Ben Gurion Sdeh Boker Field School 47 D17
Midreshet Ruppin 15 C9
Mif'alei Yam Hamelech (Dead Sea Works) 38 G15
Mifgash Habik'a (Crocodile Farm) 14 F9
Migdal 6 E4
Migdal Ha'emek 12 D5
Migdalim 14 F9
Migdal Oz 23 E12
Migdal Tefen 8 D3
Mi'ilya 8 D3
Mik'hol 31 E14
Mikveh Yisrae'el 21 C10
Mini Israel 19 D11
Mirkeh 13 E7
Misgav 5 D4
Misgav Am 1 E1
Misgav Dov 27 C11
Mishmar Ayalon 22 D10
Mishmar David 22 D11
Mishmar Ha'emek 12 D6
Mishmar Hanegev 33 C14
Mishmar Hasharon 15 C9
Mishmar Hashiva 21 C10
Mishmar Hayarden 3 F3
Mishmarot 11 C7
Mishmeret 15 C9
Mishor Adumim (Kiryat Hata'asiya) 17 F11
Mishor Ami'az 38 G15
Mishor Dover 18 G10
Mishor Haruhot 47 D18
Mishor Hiyon 52 F21
Mishor Ovil 51 F20
Mishor Paran 55 E22
Mishor Rotem 37 F15
Mishor Yamin 37 F16
Mishor Yeroham 39 E16
Misilyeh 13 E7
Mitzpa 6 E4
Mitzpeh Afek 4 G4
Mitzpeh Amram 58 G24
Mitzpeh Arnon 24 G12
Mitzpeh Aviv 8 D4
Mitzpeh Beit Saida 3 F3

83

Mitzpeh Beko'a 22 D11
Mitzpeh Bol'an ... 2 F1
Mitzpeh Dani ... 17 F10
Mitzpeh Eilot ... 10 F5
Mitzpeh Ein Gedi
24 G12
Mitzpeh Gadot ... 2 F3
Mitzpeh Gamla .. 4 G3
Mitzpeh Gilboa ... 10 E6
Mitzpeh Golani .. 2 F1
Mitzpeh Gvulot 44 B15
Mitzpeh Hamachtesh ...
37 F16
Mitzpeh Hameishar ...
51 F19
Mitzpeh Ha'on ... 3 F4
Mitzpeh Har'el . 19 D11
Mitzpeh Hayamim 5 E3
Mitzpeh Hod ... 5 E3
Mitzpeh Kabir ... 13 E8
Mitzpeh Kedem 24 G12
Mitzpeh Kochavim ...
47 D18
Mitzpeh Ma'aleh Eli ...
37 F16
Mitzpeh Masu'a ...
25 D12
Mitzpeh Midrag 29 F13
Mitzpeh Mihvar ...
24 G12
Mitzpeh Mo'av .. 29 F14
Mitzpeh Modi'in ...
22 D10
Mitzpeh Monfort . 8 D3
Mitzpeh Nahli'el ...
24 G11
Mitzpeh Netofa ... 5 E4
Mitzpeh Ofer ... 11 C6
Mitzpeh Pe'er ... 20 E2
Mitzpeh Ramon 48 E18
Mitzpeh Ramon
Landing Strip ... 48 E18
Mitzpeh Ramta ... 2 F1
Mitzpeh Revivim ...
42 D16
Mitzpeh Sayarim ...
55 F23
Mitzpeh Shalem ...
24 G12
Mitzpeh Shivta . 41 C17
Mitzpeh Shlagim .. 2 F1
Mitzpeh Vina ... 9 E6
Mitzpeh Yeriho . 18 F10
Mitzpeh Zohar .. 29 F14
Mitzpor Yishai . 24 G12
Mivtahim ... 44 B15
Mivtzar Montfort 8 D3
Mizra ... 9 E5
Modi'in ... 19 D10
Modi'in Ilit ... 19 D10
Moledet ... 10 E6
Moran ... 5 E4
Moreshet ... 5 D4
Moshevet Rishonim
6 E3
Motza ... 20 E11
Motza Ilit ... 20 E11
Mt. Carmel ... 11 C5
Mt. Ebal ... 13 E
Mt. Grizim ... 13 E8
Mt. Herzl ... 20 E11
Mt. of Beatitudes
(Monastery) ... 3 F4
Mt. of Olives ... 17 F11
Mt. Scopus ... 20 E11
Mt. Tavor ... 9 E5

Mu'askar el Arub ...
23 E12
Mu'awiya ... 12 D6
Mukhayam Fari'a ...
13 E7
Mukhmas ... 17 F10
Muhraka - see Keren
Carmel
Muqeibila ... 9 E6
Musmus ... 12 D6
N
Na'aleh ... 19 D10
Na'ama ... 1 E2
Na'an ... 22 C10
Na'aran Synagogue ...
18 F10
Nabi Hazuri ... 2 F1
Nabi Rubin ... 21 C10
Nabi Samwil ... 20 E10
Nabi Shu'eib ... 6 E4
Nahaf ... 5 D4
Nahala ... 28 C12
Nahal Ada ... 12 D6
Nahal Adami ... 6 E5
Nahal Adarim ... 31 E15
Nahal Adashim .. 12 D6
Nahal Admon ... 38 G15
Nahal Afor ... 48 E18
Nahal Afran ... 39 E17
Nahal Ahdir ... 39 E16
Nahal Akev .. 48 E17-18
Nahal Akrabim .. 37 F16
Nahalal ... 12 D5
Nahal Alexander 15 C7
Nahal Amatzyahu ...
38 G16-17
Nahal Ami'az .. 38 G15
Nahal Amitai .. 43 A15
Nahal Amos ... 23 F12
Nahal Amram .. 58 G24
Nahal Amud ... 6 E3
Nahal Anaka ... 48 E19
Nahal Anava ... 19 D10
Nahal Anim ... 31 E14
Nahala'ot (Farm) 12 D6
Nahal Arbel ... 6 E4
Nahal Ardon ... 48 E18
Nahal Arfan ... 48 E17
Nahal Arod
54-55 D-E19
Nahal Aro'er ... 31 E15
Nahal Arugot ... 23 F12
Nahal Ashalim .. 38 G15
Nahal Ashosh ... 46 F19
Nahal Atad ... 56 G21
Nahal Atadim .. 42 D16
Nahal Avdat 47 D17-18
Nahal Avid ... 5 D4
Nahal Aviya ... 38 G16
Nahal Ayalon ... 19 D10
Nahal Ayit ... 4 G3
Nahal Barak .. 52 F-G19
Nahal Bazelet ... 4 G3
Nahal Be'er Hayil ...
42 D16
Nahal Be'erotayim ...
49 C18
Nahal Be'er Sheva ...
31 E14
Nahal Beit Ha'emek
8 D3
Nahal Beko'a ... 39 D15
Nahal Ben Ya'ir . 2 G13
Nahal Besor .. 44 B-C15
Nahal Betzet ... 7 C3

Nahal Bitron ... 38 G17
Nahal Bohu ... 36 B14
Nahal Bokek .. 2 F-G14
Nahal Boker ... 42 D16
Nahal Botmim .. 55 F23
Nahal Broka ... 54 D20
Nahal Daliyot ... 3 F3
Nahal Darga ... 23 F11
Nahal Demama 52 G20
Nahal Deres ... 48 E17
Nahal Dimona ... 29 F15
Nahal Dishon ... 1 E3
Nahal Divshon . 47 D17
Nahal Dohan ... 46 G17
Nahal Ef'eh ... 37 F15
Nahal El Al ... 4 G4
Nahal Eli'av ... 53 D19
Nahal Eli'az ... 53 D20
Nahal Elitzur ... 53 D19
Nahal Enmar ... 45 F18
Nahal Erga ... 46 G18
Nahal Eshet ... 52 G20
Nahal Eshtemo'a ...
31 E13
Nahal Etek ... 58 F24
Nahal Etzi'ona .. 25 D12
Nahal Evlayim ... 5 D4
Nahal Ezuz ... 49 C18
Nahal Ga'aton ... 7 C3
Nahal Galim ... 11 C5
Nahal Gamla ... 4 G3
Nahal Gazam ... 45 F19
Nahal Ge'a ... 27 B12
Nahal Geled ... 45 F18
Nahal Gerar ... 33 C14
Nahal Gidron ... 46 F17
Nahal Gilbon ... 2 F2
Nahal Girzi ... 55 F21
Nahal Gishron .. 58 F25
Nahal Gita ... 8 D3
Nahal Golhan ... 37 F16
Nahal Gorfan ... 24 F11
Nahal Gov ... 37 F16
Nahal Govta ... 2 F1
Nahal Grofit ... 56 G22
Nahal Gush Halav ...
20 E3
Nahal Guvrin ... 25 D12
Nahal Ha'arava 38 G17
Nahal Hadav ... 45 F19
Nahal Hadera ... 15 C7
Nahal Ha'ela .. 25 D12
Nahal Hagdeira . 56 F23
Nahal Halamish . 2 G14
Nahal Hamarmar ...
38 G15
Nahal Hamdal ... 2 F2
Nahal Harduf ... 29 F13
Nahal Harod ... 9 E6
Nahal Haro'eh . 42 D17
Nahal Haroz ... 54 E20
Nahal Haruvim .. 11 C6
Nahal Hashomer . 1 E1
Nahal Hatira ... 37 F16
Nahal Hatzatz ... 39 E17
Nahal Hatzbani - see
Nahal Snir
Nahal Hatzera ... 37 F16
Nahal Hatzerim 33 C14
Nahal Hatzetzon ...
23 F12
Nahal Hatzeva ... 37 F17
Nahal Hatzor ... 1 F3
Nahal Hava ... 48 E17
Nahal Haviva ... 16 D7

Nahal Hed ... 42 D15
Nahal Heiman .. 39 D16
Nahal Heimar ... 2 G15
Nahal Hemda .. 52 G20
Nahal Heter ... 2 G15
Nahal Hever ... 24 F13
Nahal Hevron ... 31 E13
Nahal Hevyon ... 39 E16
Nahal Hilazon ... 5 D4
Nahal Himrit ... 38 G15
Nahal Hipushit 41 C15
Nahal Hiyon ... 52 F21
Nahal Horsha 4 C18-19
Nahal Hovav ... 42 D15
Nahal Idan ... 38 G16
Nahalin ... 23 E11
Nahal Isaron ... 56 F22
Nahal Iyon ... 1 E-F 1-2
Nahal Kadesh Barne'a ..
4 C19
Nahal Kadkod .. 56 G23
Nahal Kama ... 33 C14
Nahal Kamai ... 45 F18
Nahal Kana ... 13 E8
Nahal Kanaf ... 3 F4
Nahal Kana'im ... 2 G14
Nahal Kanfan ... 29 F14
Nahal Karkom .. 54 E20
Nahal Karkor ... 34 D14
Nahal Karma ... 55 F22
Nahal Kedem ... 24 F12
Nahal Keinan ... 54 E19
Nahal Kelil ... 1 F2
Nahal Ken ... 56 F21
Nahal Ketura ... 56 G22
Nahal Ketzev ... 56 F21
Nahal Ketzi'a ... 54 D19
Nahal Kevuda ... 4 C17
Nahal Keziv ... 7 C3
Nahal Kidod ... 2 F14
Nahal Kidron ... 23 F11
Nahal Kimrir ... 29 F14
Nahal Kina ... 29 F14
Nahal Kishon ... 11 C5
Nahal Kishor ... 8 D3
Nahal Kitmit ... 29 F15
Nahal Koren ... 1 F2
Nahal Koshesh .. 37 F17
Nahal Lachish .. 25 D12
Nahal Lavan ... 4 C17
Nahal Lot ... 2 G15
Nahal Lotz ... 53 D19
Nahal Ma'acah ... 1 E1
Nahal Ma'aleh .. 37 F16
Nahal Ma'azer ...
54 D-E20
Nahal Mador ... 39 E17
Nahal Makuk ... 17 F10
Nahal Malhata .. 29 F14
Nahal Malkishu'a ...
10 F6
Nahal Mamshit .. 37 F16
Nahal Marzeva .. 45 F17
Nahal Mash'abim ...
39 D16
Nahal Mashak .. 38 G17
Nahal Masor ... 46 F17
Nahal Mazar ... 38 G16
Nahal Me'arot ... 11 C6
Nahal Mefalsim 36 B13
Nahal Meishar ...
45 F18-19
Nahal Meitzar ... 4 G4
Nahal Menahem . 2 F14
Nahal Menuha . 52 G20

84

Nahal Meshek ... 46 G17
Nahal Meshushim 3 F3
Nahal Mesura ... 42 D17
Nahal Metzada .. 2 G13
Nahal Michmas . 17 F10
Nahal Migdalit . 34 D13
Nahal Milha 14 F7
Nahal Milhan ... 56 F23
Nahal Mingar 39 E16
Nahal Mis'ad 39 D16
Nahal Mishmar .. 2 G13
Nahal Mitzla'ot .. 37 F16
Nahal Modi'in .. 19 D10
Nahal Mohila 48 E18
Nahal Morag 2 F14
Nahal Na'aman 7 C4
Nahal Nahash
Hatzameh 48 E17
Nahal Namer 7 C3
Nahal Nekarot 45 F18
Nahal Netafim ... 58 F24
Nahal Netiv 25 D11
Nahal Nevatim .. 31 E15
Nahal Nitzana .. 47 D18
Nahal Nokdim .. 39 D15
Nahal Odem ... 56 G23
Nahal Ofakim ... 33 C14
Nahal Og 18 F10
Nahal Omer 46 G18
Nahal Ometz 15 C7
Nahal Oretz 38 F16
Nahal Orvim 2 F2
Nahal Oshrat 7 D3
Nahal Oz 36 B13
Nahal Paran ... 52 F20
Nahal Parsa 2 G14
Nahal Patish ... 33 C14
Nahal Peki'in 8 D3
Nahal Peres 38 G15
Nahal Poleg 15 C9
Nahal Prat 17 F10
Nahal Pratzim .. 38 G15
Nahal Qini 12 D6
Nahal Qumran .. 18 F11
Nahal Rahaf 2 F-G14
Nahal Raham .. 58 G24
Nahal Rahash .. 46 G17
Nahal Rahum 1 F2
Nahal Rakad 4 G4
Nahal Ramon ... 47 E19
Nahal Raviv 4 C17
Nahal Refa'im ... 23 E11
Nahal Refed 39 E16
Nahal Re'im 52 F19
Nahal Revivim ......
39 D-E16
Nahal Roded ... 58 G24
Nahal Rut 49 B17
Nahal Sa'ar 2 F1
Nahal Sad 33 C13
Nahal Safun 4 C17
Nahal Sagi 54 E21
Nahal Sal'it 46 F17
Nahal Samak .. 4 F-G4
Nahal Sansan 25 D-E11
Nahal Sarach 8 D3
Nahal Saraf 45 F17
Nahal Sayif 37 F16
Nahal Sdom 38 G15
Nahal Sechacha 18 F11
Nahal Secher ... 39 E15
Nahal Sfamnun . 4 F-G3
Nahal Sha'al 7 C3
Nahal Shahak .. 46 G17

Nahal Shahar 42 D16
Nahal Shaharut ....
56 F-G22
Nahal Shani 58 F24
Nahal Sharsheret ....
36 B14
Nahal Shechem .. 15 C9
Nahal Shehoret 58 G24
Nahal Sheizaf ... 46 G17
Nahal Shikma ... 33 C13
Nahal Shiloh 22 D9
Nahal Shita 52 G21
Nahal Shitim 52 F21
Nahal Shizafon .. 56 F21
Nahal Shmariya 33 C14
Nahal Shu'alim . 39 E16
Nahal Shunra ... 41 C16
Nahal Si'on 2 F1
Nahal Sira 51 F20
Nahal Sirpad 4 C18
Nahal Snir (Hatzbani) ..
1 E1
Nahal Sorek 20 E11
Nahal Sovech 45 F17
Nahal Taleh 39 E15
Nahal Tamar 29 F14
Nahal Taninim ... 11 C6
Nahal Tavor 9 E5
Nahal Te'enim .. 16 D8
Nahal Teko'a 23 F12
Nahal Tel Aviv Station .
21 C9
Nahal Teref 45 F17
Nahal Timna ... 58 G23
Nahal Tirtza (Wadi
Far'ia) 14 F8
Nahal Tov 29 F14
Nahal Trashim .. 54 E19
Nahal Tut 11 C6
Nahal Tzafit 37 F15
Nahal Tzalmon 5 E4
Nahal Tzanin 38 G16
Nahal Tzavo'a ... 39 E16
Nahal Tze'ela 56 F23
Nahal Tze'elim .. 29 F14
Nahal Tzefa 37 F15
Nahal Tzemer ... 32 E15
Nahal Tzenifim .. 55 F21
Nahal Tzihor 51 F21
Nahal Tzin 37 F16-17
Nahal Tzinim ... 48 E17
Nahal Tzipori 12 D5
Nahal Tziv'on 5 E3
Nahal Tziya 54 E19
Nahal Tzofar ... 46 G19
Nahal Tzon 42 D15
Nahal Tzvira 46 F18
Nahal Uvda 56 F23
Nahal Ya'alon ... 56 G21
Nahal Yafruk ... 54 D20
Nahal Yahav ... 46 G18
Nahal Yamin ... 37 F16
Nahal Yano'ah 8 D3
Nahal Yardinon 1 F2
Nahal Yarkon ... 21 C9
Nahal Yasif 7 C4
Nahal Yatir 31 E14
Nahal Yavne'el 6 E4
Nahal Yaziz 52 F-G20
Nahal Ye'elim .. 2 F-G14
Nahal Yehalya .. 38 G16
Nahal Yehi'am 8 D3
Nahal Yehudiya 2 G2-3
Nahal Yeroham 39 E16
Nahal Yerusha .. 38 G16

Nahal Yeter 47 D18
Nahal Yiftah'el 5 D4
Nahal Yishai 24 G12
Nahal Yitav 17 F9
Nahal Yo'ash ... 38 G16
Nahal Yokne'am ....
12 C-D5-6
Nahal Yosifon 2 G2-3
Nahal Za'af 52 F19
Nahal Zahal 39 D15
Nahal Zarhan 3 E17
Nahal Zavitan 2 G2
Nahal Zik 48 E17
Nahal Zohar 2 G14
Nahal Zro'a 37 F16
Naham 25 D11
Nahara'im 10 F5
Nahar Hayarmuk . 4 G4
Nahariya 7 C3
Nahariya Station ... 7 C3
Nahli'el 20 E10
Nahli'eli, Island 7 C3
Nahsholim 11 C6
Nahshon 19 D11
Nahshonim 22 D9
Na'in el Hamta 4 G4
Na'omi (Na'ama) ....
18 F10
Naqura 7 C3
Nataf 19 D11
National Water Carrier
6 E4
Natur 4 G4
Natzrat Ilit 9 E5
Na'ura 9 E5
Nazareth (Natzrat) ....
9 E5
Nazlat Isa 16 D7
Nazleh 36 B13
Nazlet Zeid 12 D7
Nebi Sabalan 8 D3
Nebi Yusha 1 E2
Negba 27 C12
Negba Open Museum ..
27 C12
Negev (Negeb) .. 34 D14
Negohot 34 D13
Nehalim 22 C9
Nehora 28 C12
Nehusha 25 D12
Nein (Na'im) 9 E5
Ne'ot Hadekel .. 36 B13
Ne'ot Hagolan 4 F-G4
Ne'ot Hakikar .. 38 G16
Ne'ot Kedumim Park ...
19 D10
Ne'ot Mordechai 1 E2
Ne'ot Smadar
(Shizafon) 56 G21
Neri'a 20 E10
Nes Amim 7 C4
Nes Harim 25 E11
Nesher 11 C5
Nes Tziyona ... 21 C10
Netafim Border
Crossing 58 F24
Neta'im 21 C10
Netanya 15 C9
Netanya Station .. 15 C9
Netiv Ha'asara 36 B13
Netiv Hagedud .. 18 F9
Netiv Halamed Heh ....
25 D12
Netiv Hashayara ... 7 C3
Netivot 36 B14

Netu'a 8 D3
Netzer Sereni ... 22 C10
Ne'urim 15 C7
Nevatim 34 D15
Neveh Ativ 2 F1
Neveh Avot 11 C7
Neveh Dani'el ... 23 E11
Neveh Efra'im
Monoson 22 C10
Neveh Eitan 10 F6
Neveh Harif 56 G22
Neveh Ilan 19 E11
Neveh Menahem 16 D8
Neveh Micha'el 25 D12
Neveh Mivtah ... 27 C11
Neveh Shalom .. 19 D11
Neveh Temarim ....
42 D16
Neveh Tzuf - see
Halamish
Neveh Ur 10 F5
Neveh Yam 11 C6
Neveh Yamin 15 C9
Neveh Yarak ... 22 C9
Neveh Ziv 7 C3
Neveh Zohar 2 G14
Neveh Zohar Landing
Strip 2 G14
New Hula 1 F2
Nili 19 D10
Ni'lin 19 D10
Nimrod 2 F1
Nir Akiva 33 C13
Nir Am 36 B13
Niran (Na'aran) ... 18 F9
Nir Banim 28 C12
Nir Eliyahu 15 C9
Nir Etzyion 11 C5
Nir Galim 27 B11
Nir Hen 28 C12
Nirim 35 B14
Nirit 16 D9
Nir Moshe 33 C13
Nir Oz 35 B15
Nir Tzvi 22 C10
Nir Yafeh 12 D6
Nir Yisra'el 27 B12
Nir Yitzhak 43 B15
Nisf Jubeil 13 E8
Nitzana (Educ. Comm.)
49 B17
Nitzana Border
Crossing 49 B17
Nitzanei Oz 15 D8
Nitzanei Sinai .. 49 B17
Nitzanim 27 B12
No'am 28 C13
Nof Ayalon 19 D10
Nofech 22 C9
Nofei Prat 17 F10
Nofim 16 D9
Nofit 12 D5
Noga 27 C12
Nokdim 23 F11
Nordiya 15 C9
Nov 4 G4
Nuba 25 E12
Nuclear Research
Center 21 B11
Nu'eima 18 F10
Nu'eima (Refugee
Camp) 18 F10
Nur esh Shams .. 16 D8
Nuseirat 35 A14

O

Odem 2 F1
Ofakim 33 C14
Ofarim 19 D9
Ofer 11 C6
Ofra 20 E10
Ofra Field School ....
20 E10
Ohad 44 B15
Ohalo 3 F5
Old Jaffa 21 B10
Olesh 15 C9
Omen 12 D6
Omer 34 D14
Ometz 15 C7
Ora 20 E11
Or Akiva 11 C7
Oranim 12 D5
Oranit 16 D9
Or Ganuz 5 E3
Or Haner 36 B13
Oron Phosphate
Factory 3 E16
Orot 28 C11
Ortal 2 F2
Or Yehuda 22 C10
Oshrat 7 C3
Otni'el 31 E13

P

Pa'amei Tashaz 33 C13
Palmahim 21 B10
Paran 52 G19
Pardes Hana-Karkur .....
11 C7
Pardesiya 15 C9
Park Agam Yeroham ......
39 E16
Park Alona 11 C6
Park Arad 29 F14
Park Be'erotayim ....
49 C18
Park Britania 25 D12
Park Golda 42 D16
Park Goren 7 D3
Park Hasla'im 8 D3
Park Lachish Ashdod ....
27 B-C11
Park Nahshonim 22 D9
Park Sapir 46 G18
Park Yarkon 22 C9
Patish 36 B14
Pedaya 22 C11
Pedu'el 19 D9
Peduyim 33 C14
Pehel 10 F6
Peki'in Hahadasha ....
8 D3
Pelech 8 D4
Pesagot 20 E10
Petah Tikva 22 C9
Petahya 22 C11
Petza'el 18 F9
Phosphate Terminal ....
37 F15
Pnei Hever 23 E13
Porat 15 C9
Poriya (Kfar Avoda) ......
3 F5
Poriya (Neveh Oved) ....
3 F4
Poriya Ilit 3 F5
Prazon 9 E6
Pri Gan 43 B15

Q

Qabalan 13 E9
Qabatiyeh 13 E7
Qa'en Naqb 57 F24
Qafin 16 D7
Qalandiyeh 20 E10
Qalansuwa 15 C9
Qalqilya 15 C9
Qarantal Cablecar ....
18 F10
Qarawet Bani Zeid ....
19 D9
Qarn el Hajar 24 F11
Qaryut 20 E9
Qasr el Yahud ... 18 G10
Qasr es Sir 39 E15
Qasr Khalifa 23 E12
Qatana 20 E11
Qibya 19 D10
Qira 13 E9
Qlei'a 1 E1
Qubet en Najameh ....
17 F10
Qubur Bani Isra'il ....
17 F10
Quneitra 2 G2
Quseima 49 B18
Qusin 13 E8
Qusra 13 F9

R

Ra'anana 15 C9
Raba 13 E7
Rab Talatin 20 E1
Rafat 19 D9
Rafat (S. Ramallah) ....
20 E10
Rafat Monastery ....
25 D11
Rafi'ah 43 A15
Rafi'ah Border Crossing
43 A15
Rafida 23 F11
Rafting Nahar
Hayarden 3 F3
Rahat 33 C14
Rakefet 5 D4
Rama 5 E3
Ramadin 34 D14
Ramallah 20 E10
Ramat Alma 1 E3
Ramat Barak 52 F19
Ramat Boker 42 D16
Ramat David 12 D5
Ramat Ef'al 21 C10
Ramat Gan 21 C9
Ramat Grofit 56 G22
Ramat Hadav 54 E19
Ramat Hakovesh 15 C9
Ramat Hanadiv .. 11 C6
Ramat Hasharon 21 C9
Ramat Hashofet .. 12 D6
Ramat Hovav
(Industrial Area) ....
42 D15
Ramat Magshimim ....
4 G4
Ramat Mazar 38 G16
Ramat Nafha 47 E17
Ramat Pinkas 21 C10
Ramat Rahel 23 E11
Ramat Razi'el 19 E11
Ramat Rut 4 C17
Ramat Tzofar 52 G19
Ramat Tzvi 9 E6
Ramat Yishai 12 D5
Ramat Yohanan 7 D5
Ramin 16 D8
Ramla 22 C10
Ramla Station .. 22 C10
Ram On 9 E6
Ramot 3 F4
Ramot Hashavim 15 C9
Ramot Me'ir 22 C11
Ramot Menashe .. 11 C6
Ramot Naftali 1 E2
Ramot Yisachar ... 10 F5
Ramun 17 F10
Ranen 33 C14
Rantis 19 D9
Ras Ali 8 D5
Ras Karkar 19 E10
Ravid 6 E4
Rechasim 12 C5
Reches Kidod 29 F14
Reches Menuha ....
52 F-G20
Reches Nafha 47 D18
Reches Yeroham ....
39 E15-16
Re'em Industrial Area ...
28 C11
Regavim 11 C6
Regba 7 C4
Rehelim 13 E9
Rehov 10 F6
Rehovot 21 C10
Rehovot Station .. 22 C10
Reihan 12 D7
Re'im 36 B14
Reina 9 E5
Reshafim 10 F6
Retamim 42 D16
Re'ut 19 D10
Revadim 28 C11
Revaha 28 C12
Revava 16 D9
Revaya 10 F6
Revivim 42 D16
Rihaniya 1 E3
Rimeish 8 D3
Rimonim 17 F10
Rinatya 22 C9
Rishonim Station ....
21 C10
Rishon Letziyon 21 C10
Rishpon 15 C9
River Jordan Terminal .
10 F6
Rock drawings .. 54 E20
Rogem Zohar .. 29 F14
Roglit 25 D12
Ro'i 14 F8
Roman Bathhouse ....
19 D11
Rom Hacarmel 11 C5
Rosh Ha'ayin 22 D9
Rosh Hanikra 7 C3
Rosh Hanikra Border
Crossing 7 C3
Rosh Horsha .. 53 D19
Rosh Pina 6 E3
Rosh Tur 24 F11
Rosh Tzukim .. 18 G11
Rosh Tzurim 23 E11
Rosh Zohar 29 F14
Rotem 14 F7
Rotem Industrial Park ..
37 F15
Ru'ah Midbar .. 33 C15
Ruhama 33 C13
Rujeib 13 E8
Rujm el Hiri 4 G3
Rujm en Naqa ... 24 F12
Rujum Hilal 26 E13
Rumana 5 D4
Rumana (Samaria) ....
12 D6
Rumat Heib 5 E5
Ruthenberg Power
Station 27 B12

S

Sa'ad 36 B13
Sa'ar 7 C3
Sabastiyeh 13 E8
Safa 19 D10
Safad (Tzfat) 6 E3
Safarin 16 D8
Safari Park 21 C10
Saham 4 G4
Sahek Ota 15 C7
Sajur 8 D3
Sakhnin 5 D4
Salama 5 E4
Salfit 20 E9
Salim 12 D6
Salim (Samaria) .. 13 E8
Salit 16 D8
Samar 56 G23
Samaria 13 E8
Sandala 9 E6
Saniriya 16 D9
Sansana 34 D14
Sanur 13 E7
Sapir 46 G18
Sara 13 E8
Sarid 12 D5
Sarta 19 D9
Sasa 5 E3
Sataf 20 E11
Savyon 22 C9
Sawa'id 5 D4
Science-based
Industries 34 D14
Sdeh Ayalon F. School ..
21 C10
Sdeh Boker 39 D17
Sdeh David 27 C13
Sdeh Dov 21 C9
Sdeh Eli'ezer 1 E3
Sdeh Eliyahu 10 F6
Sdeh Halamish .. 49 B17
Sdeh Hemed 22 C9
Sdeh Ilan 6 E5
Sdeh Moshe 28 C12
Sdeh Nahum 10 F6
Sdeh Nehemya 1 F2
Sdeh Nitzan 44 B15
Sdeh Tzvi 33 C13
Sdeh Uziyahu ... 27 C11
Sdeh Warburg 15 C8
Sdeh Ya'akov 12 D5
Sdeh Yitzhak 15 C7
Sdeh Yo'av 27 C12
Sdei Avraham .. 43 A15
Sdei Hemed 15 C9
Sdei Trumot 10 F6
Sderot 36 B13
Sdom (Sodom) .. 38 G15
Sdot Micha 25 D11
Sdot Yam 15 C7
Segev (Atzmon) .. 5 D4
Segev Shalom .. 34 D15
Segula 28 C12
Seida 16 D7
Seismographic Station .
58 G24
Sejera - see Ilaniya

Sfinat Hamidbar 42 D16
Sgavyon, Island 7 C3
Sha'ab 5 D4
Sha'al 2 F2
Sha'alvim 19 D10
Sha'ar Efra'im 15 D8
Sha'arei Avraham 28 C11
Sha'arei Tikva 19 D9
Sha'ar Ha'amakim 12 D5
Sha'ar Hagai Field School 19 D11
Sha'ar Hagolan 10 F5
Sha'ar Menashe .. 15 C7
Shabtin 19 D10
Shadmot Dvora 9 E5
Shadmot Mehola . 14 F7
Shadmot Sheizaf 49 C17
Shafir 28 C12
Shahaf, Island 7 C3
Shahar 28 C12
Shaharut 56 G22
Shalom Station (Tel Aviv) 21 C9
Shaked 12 D7
Shalva 28 C13
Shamir 2 F2
Shani (Livneh) ... 31 E13
Shaqra 1 E2
Sharona 6 E5
Sharsheret 33 C14
Shavei Shomron .. 13 E8
Shavei Tziyon 7 C3
She'ar Yashuv 1 F1
Sheba Medical Center .. 22 C9
Shechanya 5 D4
Shechem 13 E8
Shedema 27 C11
Shefer 5 E3
Sheikh Danun 7 C3
Shekef 25 D13
Shen Ramon 48 E19
Shetulim 27 C11
Shevut Rahel 20 E9
Shezor 5 E4
Shfar'am 8 D4-5
Shfayim 15 C9
Shibolim 33 C14
Shikmim Field School ... 27 B12
Shilat 19 D10
Shilo 20 E9
Shilo Valley 17 E-F9
Shim'a 31 E13
Shimshit 12 D5
Shlomi 7 C3
Shluhat Karkom 54 E21
Shluhat Keren ... 44 B17
Shluhat Mishlatim 19 D11
Shluhat Notza ... 52 G21
Shluhat Omer 46 G18-19
Shluhat Shaharut 56 G22
Shluhat Shiryon 2 F1
Shluhat Tzalmon 46 F18
Shluhat Tzva'im ... 10 F6
Shluhot 10 F6
Shmurat Adami 6 E5

Shmurat Almogei Eilat . 58 G25
Shmurat Alon 15 C7
Shmurat Alonei Abba . 12 D5
Shmurat Alonei Bar'am 5 E3
Shmurat Alonei Beit Keshet 9 E5
Shmurat Ar Atzil .. 8 D3
Shmurat Arbel 6 E4
Shmurat Ashdot Yagur 11 C5
Shmurat Ashosh 45 F19
Shmurat Atlit 11 C6
Shmurat Balfouriya 9 E5
Shmurat Be'er Osnat 41 C15
Shmurat Be'er Tze'elim 41 B15
Shmurat Beit Saida Yam 3 F4
Shmurat Bilton 8 D3
Shmurat Bitronot Be'eri 36 B14
Shmurat Bitronot Ruhama 33 C13
Shmurat Breichat Bar'on 2 F2
Shmurat Breichat Ga'ash 15 C9
Shmurat Breichat Timsah 11 C6
Shmurat Dekel Hadum 58 G24
Shmurat Dlavim 20 E10
Shmurat Dor Habonim 11 C6
Shmurat Ein Afek . 7 C4
Shmurat Ein Gedi .. 24 F-G13
Shmurat Ein Nimfit ... 7 C4
Shmurat Einot Givton ... 22 C11
Shmurat Einot Kaneh Ve Samar 24 F12
Shmurat Einot Orvim . 2 F2
Shmurat Einot Tzukim . 18 G11
Shmurat Einot Zarka 19 D10
Shmurat Ein Yehuda .. 10 F6
Shmurat El Al 4 G4
Shmurat Ge'on Hayarden (Hamadiya) 10 F6
Shmurat Ge'on Hayarden (Tirat Tzvi) 10 F6
Shmurat Gever . 25 D13
Shmurat Gilbon .. 2 F3
Shmurat Giv'at Eitza . 5 E4
Shmurat Giv'at Hamoreh 9 E5
Shmurat Giv'at Ruhama 33 C13
Shmurat Gva'ot Lahav . 34 D14
Shmurat Hadasim 15 C9
Shmurat Hamasrek 19 D11

Shmurat Hameyasdim . 1 F2
Shmurat Haminsara 48 E18
Shmurat Har Alon 11 C5
Shmurat Har Amasa 32 E14
Shmurat Har Atzmon 5 D4
Shmurat Har Avital 2 G2
Shmurat Harei Eilat 58 F24
Shmurat Har Gadir 14 F7
Shmurat Har Gamal 8 D4
Shmurat Har Gilbo'a 9 E6
Shmurat Har Giyora 26 E11
Shmurat Har Hakotz 5 E4
Shmurat Har Hanegev . 53-54 D-E 19-20
Shmurat Har Hatayasim 20 E11
Shmurat Har Hermonit 2 F-G2
Shmurat Har Kabir 13 E8
Shmurat Har Kamun 5 E4
Shmurat Har Meiron . 5 D-E3
Shmurat Har Nezer 1 E2
Shmurat Har Peres 4 G3
Shmurat Har Shechanya 5 D4
Shmurat Har Shipon 2 G2
Shmurat Har Tavor 9 E5
Shmurat Har Tzin 37 F17
Shmurat Haruva . 14 F8
Shmurat Helmoni'ot Yeroham 39 E16
Shmurat Hermon .. 2 F1
Shmurat Holot Agur 44 B16
Shmurat Holot Hamifratz 7 C4
Shmurat Holot Mash'abim 42 D16
Shmurat Holot Nitzanim 27 B12
Shmurat Holot Zikim ... 27 B12
Shmurat Horshat Ya'ala 10 F5
Shmurat Hotam Hacarmel 11 C6
Shmurat Hula 1 F2
Shmurat Hurshat Tal 1 F2
Shmurat Irus Ha'argaman 21 C10
Shmurat Irus Habitzot . 4 G4
Shmurat Irus Hadur 3 F3
Shmurat Irus Hanegev . 39 E15
Shmurat Irus Natzrati .. 9 E5

Shmurat Irus Yeroham .. 39 E16
Shmurat Karei Na'aman 7 C4
Shmurat Kenyon Shagor 8 D4
Shmurat Keren Carmel 11 C5
Shmurat Ketura 56 G22
Shmurat Kochav Hashahar 17 F10
Shmurat Lahav 34 D13
Shmurat Lahav Darom 34 D14
Shmurat Liman 7 C3
Shmurat Machteshim Ein Yahav 38 F-G16
Shmurat Margaliyot 1 E2
Shmurat Massif Eilat ... 55 F23
Shmurat Matlul Tzurim 5 D4
Shmurat Matzli'ah 22 C10
Shmurat Matzok Hatzinim 45 F18
Shmurat Mayanot Nuheila & Ein Barid ... 1 F1
Shmurat Me'arat Yonim 8 D4
Shmurat Metzad Abirim 8 D3
Shmurat Metzokei Hatzinim 48 E18
Shmurat Metzokei On .. 3 F4
Shmurat Metzukei Hacarmel Hama'aravi 11 C5
Shmurat Metzukei Hahe'tekim 18 F11
Shmurat Metzukei Ramim 1 E2
Shmurat Michrot Be'eri 36 B14
Shmurat Midbar Yehuda 30 F-G3
Shmurat Mitzpeh Eilot 10 F5
Shmurat Nahal Amud .. 6 E3
Shmurat Nahal Arugot 24 F13
Shmurat Nahal Beidan 13 E8
Shmurat Nahal Beit Ha'emek 8 D3
Shmurat Nahal Betzet . 8 D3
Shmurat Nahal Bezek Ili 14 F7
Shmurat Nahal Daliya Veyuvalim 12 C6
Shmurat Nahal Dishon 1 E3
Shmurat Nahal Dolev . 25 D11
Shmurat Nahalei Bohu Ugerar 36 B14
Shmurat Nahal Galim . 11 C5
Shmurat Nahal Gerar Hatichon 33 C14
Shmurat Nahal Habesor 36 B15
Shmurat Nahal Hamdal 2 F2

Shmurat Nahal Hashofet 12 D6
Shmurat Nahal Hatzor 1 E3
Shmurat Nahal Hilazon 5 D4
Shmurat Nahal Iyon 1 E1
Shmurat Nahal Kadesh 1 E2
Shmurat Nahal Kefira .. 25 D-E11
Shmurat Nahal Keziv 7 D3
Shmurat Nahal Lavan .. 4 C-D17
Shmurat Nahal Makuk 17 F10
Shmurat Nahal Me'arot 11 C5
Shmurat Nahal Meitzar 4 G4
Shmurat Nahal Misgav 1 E1
Shmurat Nahal Nesher 11 C5
Shmurat Nahal Ofakim 33 C14
Shmurat Nahal Orvim . 2 F2
Shmurat Nahal Poleg .. 15 C9
Shmurat Nahal Prat 17 F10
Shmurat Nahal Rahum 1 F2
Shmurat Nahal Sarach 8 D3
Shmurat Nahal Sheizaf 38 G17
Shmurat Nahal Shikma 33 C13
Shmurat Nahal Shiloh .. 22 D9
Shmurat Nahal Shu'ah 2 F2
Shmurat Nahal Sorek 25 D11
Shmurat Nahal Taninim 11 C6
Shmurat Nahal Tavor .. 10 F5
Shmurat Nahal Teko'a . 23 F11-12
Shmurat Nahal Tut 11 C6
Shmurat Nahal Yehi'am 8 D3
Shmurat Nahal Yitzhar 8 D4
Shmurat Nahal Zavitan 3 F3
Shmurat Nehalim Gedolim 51 F21
Shmurat Ne'ot Hakikar 38 G16
Shmurat Pura ... 33 C13
Shmurat Ramon -Geological Park 47 D-E19
Shmurat Reches Gvar'am 27 B13
Shmurat Reches Harutzim 15 C9
Shmurat Reches Hasulam 7 C3
Shmurat Reches Livnim 5 E4
Shmurat Re'im ... 36 B14

Shmurat Sansan 25 E11
Shmurat Sartaba . 14 F9
Shmurat Shimron 12 D5
Shmurat Shlulit Shipon 2 F2
Shmurat Susita 3 F4
Shmurat Tamun .. 14 F8
Shmurat Tel Anafa 1 F2
Shmurat Tel Dan ... 1 F1
Shmurat Tel Marva 8 D3
Shmurat Tel Saharon 10 F6
Shmurat Tel Yitzhak 15 C9
Shmurat Tzafririm 25 D12
Shmurat Tzaftzefet Haprat 10 F6
Shmurat Tzurei Haye'elim 24 G12
Shmurat Udim 15 C9
Shmurat Umm et Tut ... 9 E7
Shmurat Ya'ar Alona ... 11 C6
Shmurat Ya'ar El Quf .. 26 E12
Shmurat Ya'ar Hasolelim 5 D5
Shmurat Ya'ar Odem .. 2 F1
Shmurat Ya'ar Reihan .. 12 D7
Shmurat Ya'ar Suba .. 25 E12
Shmurat Ya'ar Um Safa 20 E9
Shmurat Ya'ar Yehudiya 3 F3
Shmurat Yitav ... 17 F9
Shmurat Yodfat .. 5 D4
Shmurat Yotvata (Hai Bar) 56 G23
Shmurat Zakum . 10 F6
Sho'eva 20 E11
Shoham 22 D10
Shoham Reg. Center 22 D10
Shokeida 36 B14
Shomera 8 D3
Shomrat 7 C4
Shomriya 34 D13
Shorashim 5 D4
Shoresh 19 D11
Shoshanat Ha'amakim . 15 C9
Shoval 33 C13
Shtula 8 D3
Shufa 16 D8
Shuni'ot Achziv . 7 C3
Shuqba 19 D10
Shuva 36 B13
Shuweika 16 D7
Si'ir 23 E12
Sika 34 D13
Silat el Harithiyeh 12 D6
Silat ez Zaher 16 D7
Silwad 20 E9
Sinai 49 B18
Sinai Desert 57 E-F24
Sinjil 20 E9
Sir 13 E7
Siris 13 E7
Site of Baptism .. 18 G10

Sitriya 22 C10
Ski Center 2 F1
Snir 1 F1
Sodom - see Sdom
Sodom Cave - see Me'arat Sdom
Solomon's Pillars 58 F23
Solomon's Pools 23 E11
Srigim (Li On) .. 25 D12
Sufa 43 A15
Sufa Crossing 43 A15
Suka Bamidbar .. 47 E18
Sulam (Shunem) .. 9 E6
Surda 20 E10
Surif 26 E12
Susita 3 F4
Susya 32 E13

T
Ta'amra 23 F12
Taba Border Crossing - see Eilat Border Crossing
Tafuh 26 E12
Tahanat Simha (Mekorot) 36 B13
Tal El 8 D4
Talfit 13 E9
Talmei Bilu 33 C13
Talmei El'azar .. 15 C7
Talmei Eliyahu . 44 B15
Talmei Yafeh 27 B12
Talmei Yehi'el .. 28 C11
Talmei Yosef 43 B15
Tal Menashe 12 D6
Talmon 20 E10
Tal Or 36 B14
Tal Shahar 25 D11
Taluzeh 13 E8
Tamra 9 E5
Tamra 8 D4
Tamun 14 F7
Ta'oz 19 D11
TAP Line Road .. 2 F2
Tarabin es San'a 34 C14
Tarameh 31 E13
Tarqumiya 25 E12
Tarum 25 D11
Tayasir 13 F7
Tayiba 10 E5
Te'ashur 33 C14
Tefahot 5 E4
Teko'a 23 F12
Tekuma 36 B13
Tel 13 E8
Tel Abu el Jaj .. 2 F2
Tel Achziv 7 C3
Tel Adami 6 E5
Tel Adashim 9 E5
Tel Afek (Antipatris) 22 C9
Tel Afek (Kurdana) 7 C4
Tel Agra 34 D13
Tel Akko 7 C4
Telalim 42 D16
Tel Amal (Nir David) ... 10 F6
Telamim 27 C13
Tel Arad 32 E14
Tel Arshaf (Apollonia) . 15 C9
Tel Ashdod 27 B11
Tel Ashdod Yam 27 B11

Tel Ashkaf 15 C9
Tel Ashkelon 27 B12
Tel Aviv Port 21 C9
Tel Aviv -Yafo (Jaffa) 21 C9-10
Tel Aza 36 B13
Tel Azeka 25 D12
Tel Batash 25 D11
Tel Beit Ma'acah 1 E1
Tel Beit Mirsim 34 D13
Tel Beit She'an .. 10 F6
Tel Beit Shemesh 25 D11
Tel Beit Yerah 3 F5
Tel Dan 1 F1
Tel Dotan 13 E7
Tel Eiton 34 D13
Tel el Ajul 9 E5
Tel el Beida 14 F7
Tel el Fari'a (Tirzah) 13 E7
Telem 26 E12
Tel en Nasbeh (Mitzpah) 20 E10
Tel Erani 28 C12
Tel esh Shamsiyeh 14 F7
Tel Gador 15 C7
Tel Gama 36 B14
Tel Gezer 22 D11
Tel Goded 25 D12
Tel Hadid 22 D10
Tel Hai 1 E1
Tel Halif 34 D14
Tel Hanaton 5 D4
Tel Haror 33 C14
Tel Hasi 33 C13
Tel Hatzor (Hazor) 1 E3
Tel Hesi 28 C13
Tel Jat 16 D7
Tel Kazir 3 F5
Tel Kedesh 1 E2
Tel Kedesh Hamizrahi .. 1 E2
Tel Kelech 34 D13
Tel Keshet 28 C13
Tel Kison 7 D4
Tel Kriyot 32 E13
Tel Lachish 25 D12
Tel Malhata 31 E14
Tel Malot 22 C11
Tel Maresha 25 D12
Tel Mashosh 31 E14
Tel Mikneh 28 C11
Tel Milha 33 C13
Tel Modi'in 19 D10
Tel Mond 15 C9
Tel Mor 27 B11
Tel Nagila 33 C13
Tel Narbata 15 D7
Tel Qasile 21 C9
Tel Rafi'ah Yam 35 A15
Tel Rehov 10 F6
Tel Rumeida 23 E12
Tel Sha'ar 8 D3
Tel Shaharit 10 F5
Tel Sharuhen 36 B15
Tel Shekef 28 C13
Tel Shera 33 C14
Tel Sheva 34 D14
Tel Shikmona 11 C5
Tel Shilo 20 E9
Tel Shimron 12 D5
Tel Shoket 34 D14

Tel Ta'anach ... 12 D6
Tel Taninim ... 11 C6
Tel Te'omim ... 10 F6
Tel Tzafit ... 28 C12
Tel Tziyon ... 20 E10
Tel Tzor'a ... 25 D11
Tel Yano'am ... 10 F5
Tel Yarmut ... 25 D11
Tel Yeriho ... 18 F-G10
Tel Yeshu'a ... 31 E14
Tel Yitzhak ... 15 C9
Tel Yizre'el ... 9 E6
Tel Yosef ... 9 E6
Teneh ... 34 D13
Terminal 3
-Ben Gurion Airport ...
22 C10
Theodosius'
Monastery ... 23 F11
Ti'anik ... 12 D6
Tiberias ... 3 F4
Tidhar ... 33 C14
Tifrah ... 33 C14
Tilfit ... 13 E7
Timna Mines ... 58 G23
Timna Park ... 58 G23
Timorim ... 28 C12
Timrat ... 12 D5
Tira ... 15 C9
Tirat Carmel ... 11 C5
Tirat Tzvi ... 10 F6
Tirat Yehuda ... 22 D10
Tirosh ... 25 D11
Tnuvot ... 15 C9
Tohelet ... 22 C10
Tomer ... 18 F9
Tower & Stockade site ..
10 F6
Tubas ... 13 E7
Tuba Zangariya ... 3 F3
Tulkarm ... 16 D8
Tulul Abu el Alayiq ...
18 F10
Tuqu'a ... 23 E12
Tur'an ... 5 E4
Turkish Police Fort ...
19 D11
Turmus Aya ... 20 E9
Tushiya ... 36 B14
Tuval ... 5 D4
Tverya Ilit ... 3 F4
Tzafririm ... 25 D12
Tzafriya ... 22 C10
Tzalfon ... 19 D11
Tze'elim ... 41 C15
Tzerifin ... 22 C10
Tzerufa ... 11 C6
Tzeviya ... 5 D4
Tzinim ... 48 E17
Tzin Phosphate Factory
37 F17
Tzipori ... 5 D5
Tziv'on ... 5 E3
Tzofar ... 46 G18
Tzofit ... 15 C9
Tzofiya ... 21 C11
Tzohar ... 44 B15
Tzomet Abba Hillel ...
27 B12
Tzomet Ada ... 11 C7
Tzomet Adam ... 14 F8
Tzomet Adanim ... 22 C9
Tzomet Adulam 25 D12
Tzomet Afek ... 22 C9
Tzomet Afik ... 4 G4

Tzomet Ahihud ... 8 D4
Tzomet Ahim ... 28 C11
Tzomet Ahisamach ...
22 C10
Tzomet Akko Darom ...
7 C4
Tzomet Akko Mizrah ...
7 C4
Tzomet Akko Tzafon ...
7 C4
Tzomet Almog ...
18 F-G10
Tzomet Alon ... 15 C7
Tzomet Alonim ... 12 D5
Tzomet Alumot ... 3 F5
Tzomet Ami'ad ... 3 F3
Tzomet Arad ... 29 F14
Tzomet Ari'el ... 13 E9
Tzomet Aro'cr ... 39 E15
Tzomet Ashkelon ...
27 B12
Tzomet Ata ... 11 C5
Tzomet Atarot ... 20 E10
Tzomet Avihayil .. 15 C9
Tzomet Avital ... 2 G2
Tzomet Avshalom ...
43 A15
Tzomet Aza Tzafon ...
36 B13
Tzomet Azeka ... 25 D12
Tzomet Bareket 22 C10
Tzomet Bar'on ... 2 F2
Tzomet Baruch ... 12 D5
Tzomet Bat Shlomo ...
11 C6
Tzomet Batzra ... 15 C9
Tzomet Bedek ... 22 C10
Tzomet Be'erotayim ...
15 C9
Tzomet Beit Berl . 15 C9
Tzomet Beit Dagan ...
21 C10
Tzomet Beit Eshel ...
34 D15
Tzomet Beit Ha'arava ...
18 G10
Tzomet Beit HaMeches
2 F3
Tzomet Beit Hameches
3 F3
Tzomet Beit Horon ...
19 D10
Tzomet Beit Ira ... 19 D9
Tzomet Beit Oved ...
21 C10
Tzomet Beit Rabban ...
27 C11
Tzomet Beit Rimon ...
5 E5
Tzomet Beit Saida .. 3 F3
Tzomet Beka'ot ... 14 F8
Tzomet Bental ... 2 F2
Tzomet Ben Zakai ...
21 C11
Tzomet Berechya ...
27 B12
Tzomet Betzet ... 7 C3
Tzomet Bik'at Timna ...
58 G23
Tzomet Bilu ... 22 C11
Tzomet Binyamina ...
11 C7
Tzomet Bnei Darom ...
27 C11
Tzomet Brenner 22 C11
Tzomet Daliyot ... 4 G3
Tzomet Damun ... 11 C5

Tzomet Deir el Balah ...
35 A14
Tzomet Dimona 39 E15
Tzomet Dorot ... 36 B13
Tzomet Dotan ... 13 E7
Tzomet Dror ... 15 C9
Tzomet Dvira ... 34 D13
Tzomet Eilabun ... 5 E4
Tzomet Eilot ... 58 G24
Tzomet Ein Afek ... 7 C4
Tzomet Ein Gedi ...
24 G13
Tzomet Ein Hamifratz ..
7 C4
Tzomet Ein Hashofet ...
12 D6
Tzomet Ein Hatzeva ...
38 G17
Tzomet Ein Zeitim 6 E3
Tzomet El Al ... 22 C10
Tzomet El Rom ... 2 F2
Tzomet Elyachin . 15 C7
Tzomet Eshkolot ...
27 B12
Tzomet Eshta'ol 19 D11
Tzomet Etziyona ...
25 D12
Tzomet Evlayim ... 8 D4
Tzomet Fureidis .. 11 C6
Tzomet Ga'aton ... 7 C3
Tzomet Gadot ... 2 F3
Tzomet Gama ... 36 B14
Tzomet Ganei
Hata'aruha ... 21 C9
Tzomet Ganim ... 22 C9
Tzomet Gazit ... 9 E5
Tzomet Gedera . 28 C11
Tzomet Gelilot ... 21 C9
Tzomet Gesher Lod ...
22 C10
Tzomet Gezer ... 22 C10
Tzomet Gilat ... 33 C14
Tzomet Ginaton 22 C10
Tzomet Giv'ati ... 27 C12
Tzomet Giv'at Yeroham
39 E16
Tzomet Giv'at Ze'ev ...
20 E10
Tzomet Giv'onim ...
20 E10
Tzomet Golani ... 5 E4
Tzomet Gomeh ... 1 E2
Tzomet Gonen ... 1 F2
Tzomet Goral ... 34 D14
Tzomet Gov Ga'ash ...
2 F2
Tzomet Granot ... 15 C7
Tzomet Gush Etzyon ...
23 E12
Tzomet Guvrin . 25 D12
Tzomet Gvulot ... 44 B15
Tzomet Ha'achsanya ...
3 F4
Tzomet Ha'amakim ...
12 C5
Tzomet Ha'arava ...
38 G16
Tzomet Habad ... 22 C10
Tzomet Hadasim 15 C9
Tzomet Hadera ... 15 C7
Tzomet Hadera Mizrah
15 C7
Tzomet Hado'ar ...
19 D10
Tzomet Ha'ela ... 25 D12
Tzomet Ha'emir ... 2 F2

Tzomet Hagadi . 33 C14
Tzomet Halafta ... 5 E4
Tzomet Halohem
Habeduwi ... 12 D5
Tzomet Halukim ...
39 D17
Tzomet Halutzei
Hata'asiya ... 7 C4-5
Tzomet Hamapalim ...
2 G3
Tzomet Hamat Gader ...
3 F5
Tzomet Hametzudot ...
1 E2
Tzomet Hamovil 12 D5
Tzomet Hamra ... 14 F8
Tzomet Hana (Pardes
Hana) ... 15 C7
Tzomet Hana (Deir
Hana) ... 5 E4
Tzomet Hananya ... 5 E3
Tzomet Hanasi .. 33 C14
Tzomet Hanatziv . 10 F6
Tzomet Hanegev ...
39 D16
Tzomet Hanita ... 7 C3
Tzomet Har Harif ...
53 D19
Tzomet Harish ... 15 C7
Tzomet Haro'eh .. 15 C7
Tzomet Haroshet 15 C7
Tzomet Hartuv . 25 D11
Tzomet Haruhot 48 E18
Tzomet Haruvit 28 C11
Tzomet Hasargel 12 D6
Tzomet Hasharon ...
15 C9
Tzomet Hashayara ...
7 C3
Tzomet Hashiryon 2 F2
Tzomet Hashita ... 10 E6
Tzomet Hashoftim 7 C4
Tzomet Hashomer ...
22 C10
Tzomet Hashomrim ...
12 D5
Tzomet Hasidim .. 11 C5
Tzomet Hatayasim ...
22 C10
Tzomet Hatishbi 12 D5
Tzomet Hativa Sheva ...
19 D11
Tzomet Hativat
Hanegev ... 34 D14
Tzomet Hatrurim ...
29 F14
Tzomet Hazehuhit ...
26 E12
Tzomet He'asor ... 7 C4
Tzomet Hefer ... 15 C7
Tzomet Heletz ... 27 C13
Tzomet Hevel Aza ...
36 B13
Tzomet Hilazon ... 5 E4
Tzomet Hillel Yaffe ...
15 C7
Tzomet Hiram ... 5 E3
Tzomet Hodiya . 27 C12
Tzomet Holit ... 43 A15
Tzomet Horashim ...
15 C9
Tzomet Hosen ... 8 D3
Tzomet Hulda ... 22 D11
Tzomet Imanu'el 16 D8
Tzomet Jaljulya ... 22 C9
Tzomet Julis ... 7 D4
Tzomet Kabri ... 7 C3

Tzomet Kalanit 15 C7
Tzomet Kalya .. 18 G10
Tzomet Kama .. 33 C13
Tzomet Karkur 15 C7
Tzomet Karmi'el .. 5 D4
Tzomet Karmi'el
Ma'arav 5 D4
Tzomet Katzrin ... 2 F3
Tzomet Katzrin Tzafon
2 F3
Tzomet Kelil 7 C3
Tzomet Kerem ... 20 E11
Tzomet Keshet 2 G3
Tzomet Ketura .. 56 G22
Tzomet Ketzi'ot 49 C17
Tzomet Kfar Hitim 3 F4
Tzomet Kfar Nahum .....
3 F4
Tzomet Kfar Saba
Mizrah 15 C9
Tzomet Kfar Tavor 9 E5
Tzomet Khan Yunis
Mizrah 35 A14
Tzomet Khan Yunis
Tzafon 35 A14
Tzomet Kidod 29 F14
Tzomet Kinneret 3 F5
Tzomet Kiryat Ye'arim .
20 E11
Tzomet Kishon 11 C5
Tzomet Kisufim 35 B14
Tzomet Ko'ah 1 E2
Tzomet Kochav
Hayarden 10 F5
Tzomet Komemiyut ....
28 C12
Tzomet Koranit 5 D4
Tzomet Korazim 3 F3
Tzomet Kovshim ....
34 D14
Tzomet Lachish 25 D12
Tzomet Lahavot
Habashan 1 F2
Tzomet Lehavim ....
34 D14
Tzomet Lod Merkaz ....
22 C10
Tzomet Ma'agar
Tzalmon 5 E4
Tzomet Ma'aleh
Efra'im 14 F9
Tzomet Ma'aleh Gamla
3 F3
Tzomet Ma'aleh
Shomron 16 D8
Tzomet Ma'arav
Rafi'ah 43 A15
Tzomet Ma'asiyahu ....
22 C10
Tzomet Ma'ayan Tzvi ..
11 C6
Tzomet Maccabim ....
19 D10
Tzomet Maccabim-
Re'ut 19 D10
Tzomet Magen .. 36 B15
Tzomet Maghar .. 5 E4
Tzomet Magshimim .....
4 G4
Tzomet Mahana'im ....
3 F3
Tzomet Malachi
(Qastina) 28 C12
Tzomet Ma'on ... 36 B14
Tzomet Margaliyot ....
1 E1
Tzomet Mas'ada 2 F1

Tzomet Mash'abim ....
42 D16
Tzomet Mashhad ... 9 E5
Tzomet Masmiyeh - see
Tzomet Re'em
Tzomet Masu'a 14 F8
Tzomet Mechora . 14 F8
Tzomet Megiddo 12 D6
Tzomet Mehola 14 F7
Tzomet Mei Ami 12 D6
Tzomet Meiron 5 E3
Tzomet Menuha ....
52 G20
Tzomet Metzada 2 G13
Tzomet Metzer 15 C7
Tzomet Metzukei
Dragot 24 G12
Tzomet Migdal 6 E4
Tzomet Migdal Afek .....
22 D9
Tzomet Misgav ... 5 D4
Tzomet Mishmar
Ha'emek 12 D6
Tzomet Mishmar
Hagvul 11 C7
Tzomet Mishor
Adumim 17 F10
Tzomet Mivtahim .....
44 B15
Tzomet Mivtza Horev ..
49 B17
Tzomet Modi'im .....
22 D10
Tzomet Mordechai ....
27 B13
Tzomet Moreshet 5 D4
Tzomet Nahalal .. 12 D5
Tzomet Nahal Amud
(Tzomet Kadarim) ...
6 E4
Tzomet Nahal Hadera ..
15 C7
Tzomet Nahal Tzalmon
(Darom) 6 E4
Tzomet Nahal Tzalmon
(Tzafon) 6 E4
Tzomet Nahariya .. 7 C3
Tzomet Nahshon .....
22 D11
Tzomet Narbata .. 15 C7
Tzomet Nashut 2 F3
Tzomet Natzrat Darom
9 E5
Tzomet Natzrat Tzafon
9 E5
Tzomet Navot 9 E6
Tzomet Nebalat 22 D10
Tzomet Nehora 27 C12
Tzomet Nehusha ....
25 D12
Tzomet Nemal Ashdod
27 B11
Tzomet Nes Harim .....
25 E11
Tzomet Netivot . 33 C14
Tzomet Netofa 5 E4
Tzomet Neveh Yamin ..
15 C9
Tzomet Nir Tzvi 22 C10
Tzomet Nitzana 49 B17
Tzomet Nokdim 42 D15
Tzomet Ofer 11 C6
Tzomet Ohalim 34 D15
Tzomet Olim 34 C14
Tzomet Ono 22 C9
Tzomet Or Akiva 11 C7
Tzomet Oren 11 C5

Tzomet Orha 4 G3
Tzomet Palmahim ....
21 C10
Tzomet Palyam 15 C7
Tzomet Paran 52 G19
Tzomet Pardesiya ....
15 C9
Tzomet Petza'el 18 F9
Tzomet Plugot .. 28 C12
Tzomet Poran 2 F2
Tzomet Poriya 6 E4
Tzomet Qabatiyeh ....
13 E7
Tzomet Qumran ....
24 G11
Tzomet Ra'anana 15 C9
Tzomet Ra'anana
Tzafon 15 C9
Tzomet Rafi'ah . 43 A15
Tzomet Rama 5 E4
Tzomet Ramat Hashofet
12 D6
Tzomet Ramlod Tzafon
22 C10
Tzomet Re'em
(Masmiyeh) 28 C11
Tzomet Regba 7 C3
Tzomet Re'im 36 B14
Tzomet Rimonim .....
17 F10
Tzomet Rosh Ha'ayin
Mizrah 22 D9
Tzomet Rosh Pina .. 6 E3
Tzomet Rotem 37 F15
Tzomet Ruppin 15 C9
Tzomet Sa'ad 36 B13
Tzomet Samak Kursi) ...
3 F4
Tzomet Sara 34 D15
Tzomet Savyon . 22 C10
Tzomet Sayarim 55 F23
Tzomet Sdeh Tzvi ....
33 C13
Tzomet Segula 22 C9
Tzomet Sha'ar Efra'im ..
16 D8
Tzomet Sha'arei Aza ..
36 B13
Tzomet Sha'ar Hanegev
36 B13
Tzomet Sha'ar Hefer ..
15 C9
Tzomet Shayerot
Etzyon 23 E11
Tzomet She'an 10 F6
Tzomet Shfar'am .. 8 D5
Tzomet Shilat 19 D10
Tzomet Shim'a .. 31 E13
Tzomet Shimshon .....
25 D11
Tzomet Shipon 2 F2
Tzomet Shizafon ....
56 F22
Tzomet Shluhot 10 F6
Tzomet Shmu'el 20 E10
Tzomet Shoket .. 34 D14
Tzomet Shomrat ... 7 C4
Tzomet Si'on 1 F1
Tzomet Somech ... 8 D5
Tzomet Susya .. 32 E13
Tzomet Ta'anach 12 D6
Tzomet Tapu'ah .. 13 E9
Tzomet Tarqumiya .....
25 D12
Tzomet Tavor 9 E5
Tzomet Tefen 8 D3

Tzomet Tel Adashim .....
9 E5
Tzomet Tel Akko ... 7 C4
Tzomet Telalim 42 D16
Tzomet Tel Arad 29 F14
Tzomet Tel Eshtori
10 F6
Tzomet Tel Yeriho .....
18 F10
Tzomet Tira 15 C9
Tzomet Tirtza 13 E8
Tzomet Toviya .. 28 C12
Tzomet Tzafit 37 F15
Tzomet Tze'elim ....
41 C15
Tzomet Tzemah 3 F5
Tzomet Tzerifin 22 C10
Tzomet Tzihor .. 52 F20
Tzomet Tziporim ....
47 D17
Tzomet Tzur Hadassah
26 E11
Tzomet Urim 36 B14
Tzomet Ussishkin . 7 C3
Tzomet Vulkan 11 C5
Tzomet Ya'ar Odem .....
2 F1
Tzomet Yad Rambam ...
22 C10
Tzomet Yagur 11 C5
Tzomet Yanuv 15 C9
Tzomet Yasif 7 D4
Tzomet Yavor 8 D4
Tzomet Yehud .. 22 C10
Tzomet Yehudiya .. 3 F3
Tzomet Yehud Ma'arav
22 C10
Tzomet Yeroham ....
39 E16
Tzomet Yeroham
Tzafon 39 E16
Tzomet Yesha 1 E2
Tzomet Yeshayahu .....
25 D12
Tzomet Yesud
Hama'ala 1 F3
Tzomet Yiftah'el .. 5 D5
Tzomet Yisachar .. 9 E6
Tzomet Yishai 12 D5
Tzomet Yizre'el 9 E6
Tzomet Yodfat 5 D4
Tzomet Yokne'am .....
12 D5
Tzomet Yorke'am .....
37 F16
Tzomet Yuvalim .. 5 D4
Tzomet Zemer 16 D7
Tzomet Zikim 27 B13
Tzomet Zivan 2 G2
Tzomet Zohar .. 2 G15
Tzomet Zvulun .. 11 C5
Tzor'a 25 D11
Tzoran 15 C9
Tzova 20 E11
Tzrif Rishonim ... 7 C3
Tzufim 16 D8
Tzukei Hadud .. 52 F20
Tzukei Kavarot 3 F4
Tzukei Paran .. 51 F20
Tzukei Shayarot
56 G22
Tzukei Timna 58
F-G23
Tzukei Tzihor .. 51 F21
Tzukei Uvda .. 55 F22
Tzukei Yam 15 C9

90

Tzukim (Mahaneh Bildad) 46 G19
Tzuk Tamrur 2 G14
Tzur Hadassah .. 26 E11
Tzuri'el 8 D3
Tzurit 5 D4
Tzur Moshe 15 C9
Tzur Natan 16 D8
Tzur Yigal 15 D8
Tzur Yitzhak 15 D8
Tzvi Experimental Station 18 F9

U

Ubeidiyeh 23 F11
Udaleh 13 E8
Udim 15 C9
Ugdat Haplada Memorial 43 A15
Umm Batin 34 D14
Umm el Fahm 12 D6
Umm el Ghanam ... 9 E5
Umm et Tut 9 E7
Umm Ilas 25 D12
Umm Qutuf 12 D7
Umm Safa 20 E9
Um Zuqa 14 F7
University Station (Tel Aviv) 21 C9
Upper Beit Horon 20 E10
Urif 13 E8
Urim 36 B14
USA Indep. Park 25 D11
Usarin 13 E9
Usha 12 C5
Uvda 56 F22
Uvda Landing Strip 56 F22
Uza 28 C12
Uzeir 5 E4

V

Vardon 28 C12
Vered Hagalil 3 F3
Vered Yeriho 18 F10

W

Wadi Abu Adba 57 F24
Wadi Abu Alaliq 57 F24
Wadi Abu Alirta 53 D21
Wadi Abu Bithran 57 E-F24
Wadi Abu Remithi 57 E24
Wadi Abu Sidra 14 F8
Wadi Abu Tur 57 F23-24
Wadi Abu Urgan 53 D20
Wadi Awja 18 G9
Wadi Damtha 57 F25
Wadi Dura 14 F8

Wadi el Arab 10 F5
Wadi el Arub 23 E12
Wadi el Azariq .. 44 B17
Wadi El Beida 55 E23
Wadi El Ma'in ... 53 C20
Wadi El Malaha . 18 G9
Wadi et Taiyiba ... 10 F6
Wadi Fukhin 26 E11
Wadi Haneikiya 58 F25
Wadi Hasha 55 E22
Wadi Khariza ... 53 C20
Wadi Maksarat Hasan . 55 F23
Wadi Pehami 55 E22
Wadi Qadis 4 C19
Wadi Qantara ... 52 G19
Wadi Tilah 38 G16
Wadi Umm Butma 57 E23
Wadi Umm Haluf 54 D21
Wadi Umm Hashim 49 C19
Wadi Yabis 10 F7
Waqqas 10 F6
Wazani 1 E1
Wingate Institute 15 C9

Y

Ya'ad 5 D4
Ya'alon 56 G21
Ya'ara 7 C3
Ya'ar Ahihud 8 D4
Ya'ar Bar Giyora 25 D-E11
Ya'ar Be'eri 36 B14
Ya'ar Beit Guvrin 25 D12
Ya'ar Ben Shemen 22 D10
Ya'ar Biriya 6 E3
Ya'ar Dorot 33 C13
Ya'ar Eshta'ol ... 19 D11
Ya'ar Hadera 15 C7
Ya'ar Hakedoshim 19 D11
Ya'ar Hanasi ... 25 D11
Ya'ar Harei Naftali 1 E2
Ya'ar Haruvit 28 C-D11
Ya'ar Hulda (Herzl) 22 D11
Ya'ar Ilaniya 12 D5
Ya'arit (abandoned) 16 D8
Ya'ar Kabri 7 C3
Ya'ar Kadima 15 C9
Ya'ar Kesem 22 D9
Ya'ar Kiryat Gat 28 C12
Ya'ar Ko'ah 22 D9
Ya'ar Lahav 34 D14
Ya'ar Lavi 6 E4

Ya'ar Lon 33 C14
Ya'ar Masu'a 25 D12
Ya'ar Mei Ami 12 D7
Ya'ar Mordot Natzrat .. 9 E5
Ya'ar Nahal Secher 39 D15
Ya'ar Nehusha .. 25 D12
Ya'arot Gilboa 10 F6
Ya'arot Hacarmel 11 C5
Ya'arot Hacarmel Resort 11 C5
Ya'arot Menashe 12 D6
Ya'ar Segev 8 D4
Ya'ar Tzor'a 19 D11
Ya'ar Yatir 31 E14
Ya'bad 16 D7
Yabrud 20 E9
Yad Binyamin (Educ. Cnt.) 28 C11
Yad Hana 15 D8
Yad Hashmona . 20 E11
Yad Kennedy ... 23 E11
Yad Lashiryon Mus. 19 D11
Yad Mordechai . 27 B13
Yad Natan 27 C12
Yad Rambam 22 C-D10
Ya'el 9 E6
Yafa (Yafi'a) 12 D5
Yafit 14 F9
Yafo (Jaffa) 21 C9-10
Yagel 22 C10
Yagur 11 C5
Yahel 56 G21
Yahini 36 B13
Yakir 16 D9
Yakum 15 C9
Yama 16 D7
Yanuh 8 D3
Yanun (Arab village - Jordan Valley) 14 F8
Yanun (Moshav) 28 C11
Yanuv 15 C9
Yardena 10 F6
Yardenit 3 F5
Yarhiv 15 D9
Yarkona 22 C9
Yarkon Cemetery 22 C9
Yarun 5 E3
Yashresh 22 C10
Yasir 13 E7
Yasuf 13 E9
Yasur 8 D4
Yata 31 E13
Yated 43 A15
Yatir 31 E14
Yatma 13 E9
Yatzitz 22 C11

Yavne'el 10 F5
Yavneh 21 C11
Ye'af 15 C9
Yedida 20 E11
Yedidya 15 C9
Yehi'am 8 D3
Yehud 22 C10
Yehudiya 3 F3
Yeroham 39 E16
Yesha 44 B15
Yesodot 22 C11
Yesud Hama'ala 1 F2
Yevul 43 A15
Yif'at 12 D5
Yiftah 1 E2
Yirka 8 D4
Yiron 1 E3
Yish'i 25 D11
Yitav 18 F9
Yitzhar 13 E8
Yizre'el 9 E6
Yizre'el Valley 9 E6
Yodfat 5 D4
Yokne'am (Moshava) .. 12 D6
Yokne'am Ilit 12 D5
Yonatan 4 G3
Yoshivya 33 C13
Yotvata 56 G22
Yotvata Landing Strip .. 56 G22
Yuval 1 E1
Yuvalim 5 D4

Z

Zabda 16 D7
Zabdi'el 28 C12
Zalafa 12 D6
Zano'ah 25 D11
Zarit 8 D3
Zarzir 12 D5
Za'tara 23 F11
Za'ura 2 F1
Zawata 13 E8
Zawiyeh 13 E7
Zechariya 25 D11
Zeita (south Samaria) .. 13 E9
Zeita (west Samaria) .. 16 D7
Zeitan 22 C10
Zemer 16 D7
Zerahiya 28 C12
Zeru'a 33 C13
Zichron Ya'akov . 11 C6
Zikim 27 B13
Zimrat 36 B14
Zohar 27 C12
Zoo Station (Jerusalem) 26 E11
Zubeidat 14 F8
Zububeh 13 D6